ROUGH RIDERS

ROUGH RIDERS

TWO BROTHERS
AND THE LAST STAND
AT GALLIPOLI

PETER DOYLE

For the forgotten men of Suvla Bay

First published 2015

The History Press
The Mill, Brimscombe Port
Stroud, Gloucestershire, GL5 2QG
www.thehistorypress.co.uk

Original and explanatory text © Peter Doyle, 2015

The right of Peter Doyle to be identified as the Author
of this work has been asserted in accordance with the
Copyright, Designs and Patents Act 1988.

British Library Cataloguing in Publication Data.
A catalogue record for this book is available from the British Library.

ISBN 978 0 7509 6294 0

Typesetting and origination by The History Press
Printed and bound in Great Britain by TJ International Ltd

Contents

Preface

A bundled collection of letters which chronicled the wartime histories of two brothers from Muswell Hill, a relatively well-to-do suburb of London, emerged in an antique shop. Frank and Percy Talley, Troopers 2365 and 2366 of the 1st City of London Yeomanry (Rough Riders), were educated middle-class men who volunteered for duty as 'yeomen', and who experienced what it was like to be soldiers of Britain's volunteer cavalry in the early years of the war. It was their destiny to leave the shores of England to take part in the last, and most costly, single-day battle of the Gallipoli Campaign, on 21 August 1915.

In more than 200 previously unpublished and carefully composed letters, the Talley brothers describe their training in England, and their move to the east coast to man the trenches there during the invasion scare of 1914, in the wake of its bombardment by the German Navy.

The letters are from two loving sons to their parents, and have been only lightly edited. They observe the attack of German Zeppelins at Great Yarmouth. They describe the activities of the Rough Riders in preparing for war, of their transportation to Egypt and Suez, and of their expectation that they would be used in action at Gallipoli. Anchored offshore from the peninsula, ultimately they observed the landings there and the First Battle of Krithia in April 1915, and their preparations for action in the near future.

Both brothers were later involved in what was to be the last battle of the Gallipoli Campaign in August; this is their story.

The Battle of Scimitar Hill, at once the largest, the most costly and the least successful of the Gallipoli battles; the day's gain a single trench ... the day's losses a third of the troops engaged.

A.S. Hamilton MM, *The City of London Yeomanry (Roughriders)*, 1936.

Acknowledgements

The letters of Frank and Percy Talley came to me from an antique shop in central London. It has been a privilege to recount the stories of the two men, their lives at home and in action at Gallipoli. I hope this book does them justice. I would like to thank those who have had faith in their story, and who shared my enthusiasm and interest in it.

I am grateful to Glad Stockdale who typed up the letters for me – a gargantuan task – and to Jo de Vries at The History Press for her unremitting enthusiasm.

I have called upon friends and colleagues for advice and assistance: Chris Foster for his wise counsel, Rob Schäfer for his patience (while we worked on another project together), and Paul Reed. Steve Chambers very generously allowed me to use photographs from his personal collection depicting the men of the Middlesex Hussars at Suvla (and the modern vista of Scimitar Hill); these are shown in the picture section. Paul Hewitt from Battlefields Design worked with me on the maps. Julian Walker sourced newspaper references for me, which was very valuable. Hugh Petrie, in the local studies department of Hendon Library, similarly assisted me in a search for obscure newspaper references. The Antiques Storehouse, Portsmouth, kindly supplied the image of the Rough Riders' pre-war uniform. In good faith I have endeavoured to seek out copyright holders.

Finally, my biggest thanks are reserved for my greatest supporters, Julie and James.

The Rough Riders

The City of London Yeomanry (CLY) was special. While many volunteer cavalry regiments were created during the Napoleonic Wars, the CLY was raised as part of the Imperial Yeomanry in support of the Empire during the Anglo-Boer War of 1899–1902. With the war in South Africa demanding new tactics, the mounted infantryman came into his own, and new units were raised to counter the Boer threat.

Originally styled the 'County of London Yeomanry', very soon the new regiment aligned itself with the City – that square mile of financial institutions that was the hub of Empire – and adopted the suitably dashing and fashionable designation as 'Rough Riders' (RR), after the style of Theodore Roosevelt's volunteer cavalry that had stormed San Juan Hill in Cuba in 1898 during the Spanish-American War. Like many yeomanry regiments, the CLY (RR) soon became a favoured club of City men who had a penchant for equines – of officers who liked to ride to hounds in the shires, and of other ranks drawn from the various trades that dealt with horses.

Dazzled by the uniform of purple and slate blue, developed after the style of the lancers with traditional 'chapska' helmet and lancer plastron tunic, others were attracted by the possibilities available on 'walking out', and the chance of gathering the admiring glances of ladies in parks and on promenades, not to mention their annual parade as part of the Lord Mayor's Show through the City of London.

Whatever the attractions, the 1st City of London Yeomanry (Rough Riders) indeed became a force to be reckoned with during the Boer War, when, now clad in cotton khaki drill and cork helmet, the regiment was thrust into action. For this service the CLY was awarded the first of its battle honours, honours that would later be supplemented by others in the Great War – gained over a terrain in the Middle East that was not too unlike that first experienced in South Africa.

Following the South African War, the CLY (RR) formed one of the fifty-five yeomanry regiments that would become assimilated into the new Territorial Force created by Viscount Haldane in his reforms of the British Army – again in the wake of the experiences of the Boer War, when it was realised that the army would need some significant reorganisation if it ever wanted to fight a large-scale war again. Men of the volunteer, part-time, Territorial Force were designed to be home defence units, but with the arrival of a war that soon spread beyond the confines of Europe in 1914, the part-time yeomen would be asked to take the 'Imperial Service Commitment' that would take them overseas to face 'Johnny Turk' in Egypt and Gallipoli in 1915.

Frank and Percy Talley were brothers destined to serve in the ranks of the Rough Riders. Born within the City of London itself, they worked in its financial institutions – as did their father, head of a household that boasted a domestic servant in the fashionable north London suburb of Muswell Hill.

George Talley was of advanced years when his sons went to war. Originally from Portsmouth, for most of his working life he had worked in the City of London, living at its heart in Old Broad Street, just south of London Wall. Both boys were born here. An ancient part of the city, this road had been at the heart of the cutting-edge communications serving the submarine cable industry that had been born in the mid part of the nineteenth century, after the discovery of the value of gutta-percha, a natural rubber material, as an insulating material over a copper core. Laying submarine cables was big business, and by 1914 there were 322,000 nautical miles of cable laid, which enabled telegraphic communications across the globe.[i] This industry meant that George was able to support his large and growing family that would amount to six sons and two daughters. Of these, only Frank and Percy would see service in the First World War.

In 1910, Muswell Hill was a very fashionable suburb of London, the epitome of Edwardian style. Largely constructed between 1896 and 1914, the area was well planned and laid out, meeting the expectations and aspirations of the commercial classes who worked in the bustling centre of the City of London. It was constructed by the builders and developers James Edmondson and William Collins, who, amongst others, were working to take advantage of the sale of large estates to construct their Edwardian show suburb. They built fine rows of Edwardian villas arranged in curving avenues, the area ringed by green open spaces with the attractions of Alexandra Palace – built as a pleasure palace – on the hilltop to the north.

The area was prosperous. The Woodlands Estate that contained the Talleys' home was built on the site of a large house and 'pleasure gardens' that was sold in 1890 for development. By 1905, the developer R. Metherill had built 'solid substantial Edwardian houses, with two storeys at the front and three behind' houses in Woodland Rise – houses that retailed at a handsome £550.[ii] It was to this brand-new, leafy street, that took its name from the ancient woodlands of Highgate Wood and Queen's Wood, that George Talley and his wife Sarah moved in his retirement, together with his youngest children, Alice, Percy and Frank.

Still living with his parents in 1910, Percy Lima Stanley was 22½ years old and was working in the City of London as a clerk in the stock exchange. At the outbreak of war, he was 26 years of age and was the smaller of the two brothers, standing at 5ft 4in, at a time when the average height of the British soldier was 5ft 5in – and the minimum acceptable requirement was 5ft 3in. He was described as of good physical development and fit, although he had suffered from kidney issues some two years before joining – problems that would return.

Frank Leslie Talley also gave his parents' address on attesting to join the Rough Riders, when both brothers made their commitment to join on 27 August 1914 at the wartime home of the regiment in Putney. Frank was 28 and had already served four years as a Territorial 'Saturday night' soldier. He was taller than his younger brother, standing at 5ft 7in. Joining the 3rd London Brigade of the Royal Field Artillery at the age of 22½ years in February 1909, he emerged as '479 Driver Frank Leslie Talley'.

In the early part of the twentieth century the Royal Regiment of Artillery was divided into the Royal Horse Artillery, which accompanied the cavalry as the 'Galloping Gunners'; the Royal Field Artillery, the 'Gunners', who deployed the field guns; and the Royal Garrison Artillery, the 'Heavy Gunners', who were siege gunners, capable of taking on fortifications with their heavy howitzers. Serving with the Gunners, Frank Talley worked with horses in teams of six, that would haul field guns like the 18-pounder, the principal field gun of the British Army, each pair of horses having a driver, and Frank was trained to handle this position. Frank served his time as a Territorial (nicknamed the 'Terriers'), achieving the standard required of him, and attending the annual summer camps, in Okehampton, Bordon, Salisbury and Swanage, that were so much a part of the Terrier's life. Having served the requisite amount of time, he was discharged from service exactly four years later, on 11 February 1913 – and just over a year before the world would be thrown into conflict.

As Frank was a time-expired Territorial soldier, there is little doubt that this experience must have played a part in the decision of both brothers to volunteer for service in August 1914. The Rough Riders were undoubtedly more glamorous than the artillery, and with their peacetime headquarters located in Finsbury Square – just half a mile away from their childhood home of Old Broad Street – the brothers would have been aware of the gloriously attired yeomen in their lancer uniforms who paraded through the City of London as part of the Lord Mayor's Show (as their successors still do today).

Though the headquarters of the regiment was in the fine apartments of Finsbury Square (moved from the Guildhall in 1907), their riding school and stables were established in the residential street of Lytton Grove, Putney, and paid for in part by the London livery companies and the City Corporation, as well as other, private, benefactors. Here, the peacetime complement of horses was maintained; just enough to form a nucleus of the full regimental requirement on embodiment. These horses were a local attraction, hired out and earning revenue for the regiment. There were too few horses to serve as mounts for all of the volunteer cavalrymen at their annual camps – held at Salisbury Plain from 1912 onwards – and good mounts had to be hired locally. With the coming of war and the embodiment of the regiment, this shortfall had to be made good by the regiment purchasing more mounts.

For many peacetime Rough Riders, the commitment to serve meant an annual responsibility to attend training camp. In the summer of 1914, the regiment was based at Worthing in East Sussex – a popular site for Territorial training camps. Though the early days of August were cooler than those of July, it was sunny and rain unexpected. With the summer camp having a holiday atmosphere, and the August Bank Holiday looming, the deterioration of the international situation must have come as a surprise to many, and the normal diet of training, exercise and military practice was interrupted.

And so it was that on Sunday 2 August 1914, Lieutenant Colonel O.E. Boulton TD (Territorial Decoration), commanding officer of the City of London Yeomanry, addressed the assembled ranks at their drumhead service, giving them his opinion on the darkening scene, and asking them to volunteer for overseas service. The next day, the camp was cut short at reveille:

Camp was to be struck at once. During the morning the horses were taken back to the railway and sent back to the contractors who had supplied them ... In that afternoon, with their gay Lancer uniforms of slate-blue, purple and gold packed away for good, the men marched down the road again, between crowds of cheering holiday makers ... On arrival in London, the Regiment was dismissed to await orders.[iii]

The following day, Tuesday, 4 August 1914, war was declared, and the whole Territorial Force was embodied for service, by proclamation of the King:

> We do in pursuance of the Reserve Forces Act, 1882, hereby order that Our Army Reserve be called out on permanent service, and We do hereby order the Right Honourable HERBERT HENRY ASQUITH, one of Our Principal Secretaries of State, from time to time to give and when given to revoke or vary such directions as may seem necessary or proper for calling out Our Army Reserve or all or any of the men belonging thereto.
>
> George R.I. [iv]

With war commenced, the Rough Riders busied themselves with preparations for active service. While the British Expeditionary Force of six regular divisions was being assembled prior to their movement onto the Continent, the City's yeomen took stock of their situation. Instead of the more normal four squadrons, there were to be only three, 'A', 'B' and 'D', themselves subdivided into troops. Filling these troops with an adequate number of men was challenging initially as many were exempt from service, and new recruits were needed. Men were recalled to service, and others with a military background were also recruited to fill the numbers.

Supplied by the local Territorial Association, finding uniforms for the new men was a struggle, and the issue of 'part-worn' outfits was the norm, as was the issue of the standard leather 1903 pattern equipment used by mounted troops, which consisted of belt and ammunition pouches, while the leather bandolier worn across the chest that accompanied this would have to wait. Finding horses was also a struggle. The army remounts service was hungry for suitable mounts and regimental agents scoured a list of suitable suppliers for appropriate animals.

The Rough Riders decamped from their City headquarters and relocated to their riding stables in Putney – a temporary location before the regiment finally moved on 11 August 1914, some 8 miles westwards to the late eighteenth-century cavalry barracks that adjoined Hounslow Heath. This move was significant; here was concentrated the London Mounted Brigade, comprising the 1st County of London Yeomanry (Middlesex Hussars), the City of London Yeomanry (Rough Riders), and the 3rd County of London Yeomanry (Sharp Shooters), together with attached artillery from the Honourable Artillery Company ('A' Battery), a Royal Engineer signal troop, an Army Service Corps company, and a Royal Army Medical Corps field ambulance. These units would serve together throughout the war.

Life at Hounslow was a waiting game, the regiment housed in bell tents. The Horse Purchasing Officers continued their searches, while training was invariably dismounted. It was at Hounslow that the men of the London Mounted Brigade were invited to sign the Imperial Service Commitment. With the yeomanry part of the Territorial Force, and therefore having no obligation to serve overseas, signing the Commitment meant that they would serve wherever the army wished to send them.

For most, this would mean Egypt, Gallipoli and the Middle East as part of the 2nd Mounted Division, a yeomanry cavalry formation that was raised at the close of August under Major General William Peyton. For those refusing to sign, or barred from doing so by dint of German heritage, it meant a return to the riding stables at Putney. As new recruits, the Talley brothers were not drawn into this flurry of activity at the opening of the month. Joining at the end of August 1914, they had to seek out the regiment at Putney, as the Finsbury Square address had been closed down for the duration of the war.

With the British Army reliant on volunteer recruits for most of its history, on 5 August 1914 the new Secretary of State for War, Lord Kitchener, set to work ensuring that there would be an expandable army structure to receive them. For him, the future of the army was in the creation of a 'citizen army' – the New Army of 100,000 volunteer tranches that would eventually lead to the creation of new 'service battalions' of the county infantry regiments, an ever-expanding number of new units.

In Kitchener's view, the Territorial system, developed in 1908 to provide home defence, was not capable of such rapid expansion. Nevertheless, each Territorial battalion, also part of the county infantry regiment, was given orders to duplicate. This meant that the 'first line' Territorials could draw upon the 'second line' Territorials – based at home – for recruits and drafts.

While the mounted yeomanry regiments (typically 550 men, roughly half of a single infantry battalion) were not directly comparable to their infantry brethren, they too were ordered to duplicate for the same reasons, the likelihood being an acute shortage of men as the war took its course. And so it was that joining the 1/1st City of London Yeomanry was the entirely new 2/1st City of London Yeomanry – created from scratch at Putney in August 1914, completely without horses or arms with which to train. This would become the Talleys' temporary home.

On 27 August 1914, Percy and Frank Talley reported to Lytton Grove, Putney, in order to join the Rough Riders. With regimental numbers one digit apart, they formed up next to each other in the line of potential recruits. Accepted into one of the more glamorous mounted regiments of the British Army, they set to training for their eventual active service that would take them to the shores of the Gallipoli Peninsula, and one of the most costly battles of the whole sorry campaign.

Notes

i.   Commercial Cable Company, *How Submarine Cables are Made, Laid, Operated and Repaired*, 1915.

ii.   Jack Whitehead, *The Growth of Muswell Hill*, 1995, p.101.

iii.   A.S. Hamilton MM, *City of London Yeomanry (Roughriders)*, 1936, p.6.

iv.   Royal Proclamation, 4 August 1914.

2

Home Service

The formation of the London Mounted Brigade at the cavalry barracks at Hounslow in August 1914 was significant. By this time, the regular units of the British Army were being deployed overseas. There was not only the battlefront in France and Flanders to support, there was also Britain's widespread imperial commitments to protect from the tendrils of German influence. There could only be so many regular infantry divisions, and clawing back regular infantry battalions from outposts meant replacing them with Territorials. Kitchener's New Army would take months, if not years, to come to a fully trained and operational status – and there would be no additional volunteer cavalry units raised. The responsibility for mounted actions would fall upon the shoulders of the two regular cavalry divisions, and on the reserve cavalry – the yeomanry.

Each infantry division had its share of attached cavalry, and in many cases these were yeomen. There were three regular cavalry divisions, and two regular Indian Army cavalry divisions, all of which had landed in France and Flanders by the close of 1914. The traditional role of cavalry was to provide advanced reconnaissance – the eyes of the army – probing positions in advance of the infantry, as well as spearheading attacks in the charge, routing the enemy with the force of their momentum and in the face of the sword or lance. Yet they were also to provide mobile, mounted soldiers who would fight on foot. And it was in this role that the yeomen were adept. They were grouped into mounted divisions – so named in recognition of their work in the Anglo-Boer War – and there were four mounted divisions in total, with only the 2nd Mounted Division seeing active service as a formation. The others served to supply brigades or drafts overseas, or remained on home service.

The journey from England to Gallipoli.

The yeomen of the 4th London Mounted Brigade left the cavalry barracks in Hounslow, on 29 August, to applause. Though they were no longer clad in their showy uniforms of old, the khaki figures mounted on their warhorses must have looked impressive. They were en route for Streatley, a village some 45 miles west of Hounslow, and a camp in the Chiltern Hills. The two-day march was trying for soldier and horse alike, and several animals had to be destroyed as unfit for further service – the first casualties of the Rough Riders' war.

Streatley was where war training started in earnest, training that was enacted alongside other units of the 2nd Mounted Division. Here, in the green Berkshire countryside, were brought together men of the English shires who would ultimately go on to serve together in the parched landscapes of the Middle East and the shores of Gallipoli – men of the 1st (South Midland), the 2nd (South Midland) and the 3rd (Notts and Derby) mounted brigades.

For the City men of the Rough Riders, the training was hard, with much attention given to the horseflesh that would become their mounts. Both men and horses deemed unfit for active service overseas were weeded out and replaced by those who had joined the 2nd Rough Riders at Putney. It was in one of these drafts that the Talley brothers arrived in D Squadron on 11 October, having taken the Imperial Service Commitment the month before. When they arrived, they found their squadron had been quarantined, as on 18 September one of the horses had contracted a highly infectious glandular disease ('glanders'), which had the ability to jump from species to species. With two more horses identified as having the disease, they were destroyed, and both the remainder of the horses and the men of D Squadron were isolated on the opposite bank of the Thames, at South Stoke, in Oxfordshire. The squadron only returned to the regimental fold on 11 October 1914, having missed a divisional inspection by the King and Lord Kitchener on 8 October. With the Rough Riders billeted across the region for the winter, D Squadron returned to South Stoke to be accommodated in the Malt House on 18 October.

Throughout this period, training included fitness, musketry and riding skills. Raised as mounted riflemen in the Boer War, the Rough Riders were expected to be proficient in the use of the Short Magazine Lee–Enfield, the same rifle used by all British soldiers of the day, and designed to be equally effective as an infantry rifle and as a cavalry carbine. But, significantly, on 14 October the regiment was symbolically converted from mounted soldiers to cavalrymen. From this point onwards the men were trained in the use of the 1908 pattern cavalry sword, reputedly the finest cavalry sword ever produced. Straight and true, the sword was a formidable piece of steel with a basket hilt that was designed for thrusting and the cavalry charge.

These newly acquired and carefully honed skills would nevertheless be held in abeyance once the Londoners boarded their ship bound for Gallipoli. The Talley brothers, newly attested yeomen, describe their lives in these heady weeks before action would come their way.

3 October 1914

My dear Mother

I am sorry not to have written a letter before this but our odd moments are not many and then is always plenty to do; however, the parson of this village (South Stoke) has put the village hall and schoolroom at our disposal for letter writing and games, also supplying note paper and envelopes which has made things very much more comfortable for us.

We are both feeling very fit and well, I think Percy has shaped down to camp life very well and I certainly think he is the better for it.[1] We have both got our horse blankets and keep quite warm at night and on the whole sleep well.

The country round here is very pretty hilly and woody in parts with plenty of open space for good hard gallops.

Ever your own son

Frank

---

1   Percy was prone to pain from a suspected kidney stone – a condition not spotted on enlistment, and one that would play up in the exacting conditions of the Dardanelles.

4 October 1914

My dear Parents,

Today, we have been to church 9.30 out 10.30 then we took horses
to water, and have just been paid 8/2. We got up at 6 today,
an hour later than usual. First we water horses and clean stables,
then breakfast and wash if there is time. From about 9 till 1 we
are riding - which I can tell you is very hard work, riding horse
back with rifle, dismounting with it, along fire five and then
back and mount it is so tiring. About 12.30, we water horses again
then lunch (stew every day), then rifle instruction, then horses
again at 5, then tea. We finish about 7 o'clock, then of course
there are fatigues and extras, so you see we do not have much time.
My hands are the limit, I won't discourse on them.[2] I am feeling
fit, although tired at times, I have not slept much at night.
I must own the work is jolly rough. I was on stable guard the
other night, a rotten job from 11pm till 2am. We have to watch the
horses, to see they do not break loose, they kick, bite and fight.[3]

Ever your loving son

Percy

---

2   The rough life of the horse soldier must have played havoc with the soft hands of the City worker.

3   As Percy would find out to his detriment in Egypt.

8 October 1914

Thank Father for his letter received on Sunday. We had quite a nice quiet day with Church Parade at 9.30 in the little village church. Percy is on horse guard tonight, I was on yesterday, this is our second since we came down. The weather still continues fine although the last two days have been cloudy, as soon as the weather does break we shall probably go into billets which have all been arranged.[4]

Love to all

Frank

---

4   At the Malt House in South Stoke, which still stands and is a Grade II listed building.

12 October 1914

My dear Parents,

We came over to Streatley yesterday and we are now here with the brigade. The latest rumour is that we move off to Southampton Monday week to be in readiness to cross over to France; but do not believe anything until we find ourselves actually on the move, as we have a new rumour every day. The Germans seem to be making headway, worst luck.[5] I hope Dr Lejeane is safe, what is the Belgian boy like?[6] It is very nice being at Streatley, for such things as we can get a good wash now and then. I had one today, washed in detachments down by the river, the second time I have had my pants off in two weeks, my word I am not so particular now. You ought to see me at times, hands absolutely filthy eating my fruit. I should so like to get home and see you all, but we have been told leave has been practically stopped. We have to consider ourselves finished with home, but we might have 48 hrs granted[7] but after that finished.

Ever your loving son

Per

---

5   The Battle of Flanders had commenced the day before, part of the German attempt to turn the left flank of the Allies; it would culminate in the First Battle of Ypres where the British stood firm in the face of a significant German assault.

6   At this time, Belgian refugees were pouring in to Britain, and were taken in by families who were able to give them food and shelter. It became fashionable to house Belgians in some quarters, though this fashion waned in 1915, when it became apparent that the war would not be a short one. The Talley family had evidently taken in a number of people who had fled Flanders.

7   Forty-eight-hour leave passes.

13 October 1914

My dear Mother

I hope you received my letter written on Sunday. I quite intended to ask you to also include one or two pieces of clean rag for wiping our plates and knives on, if you have already sent the rest it does not matter.

I had a line from May[8] this morning and she said that you had had six Belgians, if so I am afraid it will mean a lot of extra work for you.

I hope the rumour that I mentioned did not upset you too much,[9] although I said I did not believe it. I really don't know what to think, today they have had swords sent down for us, so it looks like business.

Whether we shall get leave or not, is another thing which we don't know, I shall be terribly disappointed if I have to go without seeing you all and I know you all will be, and also May, it seems ages since we were all together.

You remember one day I said that I should get married if I went out to the front, but you only laughed and took it as a joke, but I really should like to if it can be arranged and I can get leave, but everything is horrible uncertain and things will have to be left as they are for the time being.

We have both in fact had a third blanket issued so we are quite snug.

Love, your affectionate Son

Frank

---

8   May was his fiancée.

9   It had been rumoured that the regiment was to proceed to France and Flanders.

17 October 1914

My dear Mother and Father

We have been to the railway station to send home dirty clothes which you might wash for us and keep until we write you, as we go into billets tomorrow and at present do not know our new address. The vest you sent I am not wearing and have returned it on top of kit bag, but socks, pants and shirt will be all I shall require. Frank will still wear his vest. Such a lot of troopers were leaving for home tonight, we felt quite sick not being one of them. We are both quite well.

We have also returned our lounge coats which are very much in the way and we are not supposed to have. I had a rotten experience last night on guard and I had to guard over old rifles quite a distance from our lines. The guards were for 2 hours, and we did it quite alone. I went on at 8 till 10, then 2 till 4, at 3 o'clock somebody fired, and then horses started to stampede, officers came out shouting and firing orders. I thought the Germans had come, I was alone in a dark field while all this was going on; at 4 o'clock everything was quiet.

Please send things back in kit-bag when we write you. How is Marguerite and Lily, have they heard anything of the Dr? Please thank Harry[10] for the tobacco he sent me, and give him my love. We shall have to be moving in about 20 minutes, so will say good bye with oceans of love to all.

Ever your loving son

Percy

---

10   Harry was one of their older brothers.

18 October 1914

1 Lathbury Road
Oxford

My dear Mother and Father

Yesterday I had to go into Reading with more cart horses,
but had to ride back again so in all the distance was about
23 miles but did not feel very tired afterwards. While we
were going to Reading the other fellows were striking camp
as we went into our billets, we are in a disused cottage at
South Stoke the little village near our camp ... we are very
comfortably situated and can now, thanks to a pump, get plenty
of washing water which is a great treat, the dame in the next
cottage will give us a can of hot water after each meal for
washing our plates, etc. The horses are all in a barn about 1
minute walk away, and I am glad to say that at present we have
not to do any night guard and shall not have to unless they
kick up a row and generally make a nuisance of themselves.

Now with regard to marrying before going abroad, I am sorry
that you should have all taken such a strong objection to it.
Firstly we are not so young as we would like to be and could
afford to wait, and I think we shall neither be any the worse
off when I come back. As regards May, she has to be kept and
Mr Howell[11] is quite prepared to do it after we are married,
as he has done up to the present. Should I not return, May,
I know would rather be left as you have termed it 'a young
widow' than otherwise; it will make us both considerably
happier if we are married and I am sure to get into something
quickly on my return and the fact of being married will make it
easier. May on the other hand will be getting an allowance of
12/- per week, which will also be an advantage.[12]

---

11 May's father.
12 They married in Muswell Hill on 27 October, having obtained permission from the
    military authorities.

Percy has said something about leave to our officer for the next weekend so it may all have to be fixed up very quickly so I do hope that you will fall in with my views.

I have asked Harry to buy on my behalf a new waterproof, more after the style of a southwester as the old one I brought down with me lets as much rain as it keeps out, the price should not be more than 21/- and I should be glad if you could settle with him for me, and I will let you have it when I get back pay which is still owing.

Our new address is

Tpr F.L. Talley
'D' Squadron (No 4 Troop)
City of London Yeomanry
(Rough Riders)
South Stoke
Nr Goring Oxon

20 October 1914

My dear Mother and Father

Thank you so much for the birthday present it is very good of you during such times. We left 7.45 this morning to finish a sham fight we started the other day, we returned about 5pm such a long day. I have got a dear of a horse, a chestnut, the only thing is he changes step now and then, which is awkward, but think he will soon get out of it. The cottage we are in is quite nice, quite large rooms. We are on the ground floor, and have a grate. We have lit a fire of wood today, we hope to get some coal. I do not sleep on the hard floor so well, I don't seem to get any sleep. I have got a nasty pain under my ribs have mentioned it to one or two fellows and they say it is indigestion.[13] I think it is so, but it has been playing me up otherwise I am quite fit. I do hope you are all well at home, I think of you all at night during the day you do not have time to think of anything. Yesterday I had my first shave for about four days. My word I did look a sight. You might send our clean underclothes as soon as possible. Shall try to have the others cleaned down here to save the trouble of sending them home. How is Marguerite and Lily?[14] Please give them my love. Please do not send my vest, only pants shirt and socks. Frank wants his vest.

Ever your loving son

Percy

---

13 Caused by kidney stones, in fact. This would flare up on active service.

14 Belgian refugees staying with the Talley family. The 4 September issue of the local *Finchley Press* reported 'refugees from the alarmed town of Antwerp have arrived in Finchley, and are disclosing stories that would make one's blood run cold'.

1 November 1914

South Stoke

My dearest Mother

I am sorry not to have written you before, but we have had a somewhat busy time since I got back,[15] drawing new kit and military saddles, etc., so today has been really my first chance of writing.

You will see by the address that we are still here which is due to our not having all our equipment.[16] We shall be here definitely until Thursday this week, but after that we may have to move off working 12 hours after receipt of notice.

You will remember Percy mentioned a little row I had or rather our Sergeant had with me, I told you at the time that it was nothing and all would be right when I came back, this has turned out as I said and we quite in good terms with one another.

Yesterday we were inspected in full marching order and I am giving you a list of the things we have to take.

<u>On the Horse</u>
Cloak Rolled in front of Saddle
Sleeping Blanket rolled in macintosh
Shirt rolled at back of saddle
Mess tin   in one side of cloak
Grooming kit " other "   "   "
Sword
Rifle
2 spare horse shoes and nails
2 picketing pegs attached to sword scabbard
And 2 ropes for picketing

---

15 Frank had married his sweetheart, May Howell, in St James' Church, Muswell Hill, on 27 October. This was done against the advice of his parents.

16 Equipping the embodied Territorial Force was a challenge for the local Territorial Associations, in the face of competing pressures from both the Regular and New armies.

On the Man
Haversack containing holdall with knife, fork, spoon, razor,
comb tooth brush
1 pair socks
Waterbottle
Bayonet
Belt
Bandolier
100 round of ammunition
Under the saddle 1 Blanket for the horse and a second
for ourselves

This practically all we carry but it is bit of a job to climb
into the saddle and out again but we should soon get use to it.
  Today we draw spare tunic and riding breeches from stores,
they are not exactly a fit, but it is better to have them to
fall back on than nothing.
  Ever your affectionate son

Frank

11 November 1914

South Stoke

My dear Father

Thanks for your letter today and also for stamps enclosed.
Will you also thank Mother for the chocolate received yesterday, it was most acceptable.

Today has turned out very windy and rainy real November
weather. We are, however, very lazy in our billet, which has
not been condemned.

Our sergeant has bought an oil lamp for our room, which is a
great improvement, Percy has bought some cocoa and condensed
milk and have just made ourselves a cup, it is very comforting
in this weather and warms one up.

It is good news about the Emden and Koeningsberg[17] I think.
Soon we shall be getting them on the run, I don't suppose we
shall be back before Xmas but think we might soon after if
things take a decided turn.

News is very scarce just at present and there is nothing of
importance to tell you. I am sorry the letter is short but I know
you will be glad to get it, to hear we are still fit and well.
It is possible some photograph of our regiment may appear in some
of the daily papers, has we had them taken on Monday we should
both be in the front row if it is possible to recognise anyone.

Your affectionate son

Frank

---

17   The German cruiser SMS *Emden* was a thorn in the side of the British, and roamed
      freely with apparent immunity in the Indian Ocean, sinking British commerce
      vessels, and even bombarding Madras. The ship was run aground in the Battle of the
      Cocos on 9 November 1914 by HMAS *Sydney*. SMS *Königsberg*, another German
      cruiser and Indian Ocean commerce raider, was the target of a concerted effort by
      the British to destroy her from October 1914 when she was trapped off the coast of
      German East Africa.

13 November 1914

My dear Parents

   The chocolate you sent was simply grand, it has been quite
a meal to me at times when out on the march. The news here
is just the same continual work, tomorrow our troop are
having a dinner in the evening. Please give my love to Madame
Marguerite and Lily.[18] Today has been perishing, we had to
stand for about an hour and half in a field and all of us were
nearly frozen, the horses very restless. Tomorrow, Saturday,
we have a very big scheme[19] on. The other evening we attacked
the Middlesex.[20] I thoroughly enjoyed it, except coming home
I was dead beat and could hardly keep awake on my horse.
We arrived home about 12.30 going to bed about 2pm, up at the
same time in the morning.

   Ever your own son

   Percy

On 17 November 1914, the Rough Riders received orders to move. There
was great excitement – here at last was the chance to cross the Channel and
join the regulars in action. The first London Territorials, the 1/14th (County
of London) Battalion (London Scottish) had already crossed on 16 September,
and were in action at the end of October in the fiercely raging First Battle of
Ypres, near Messines. It was not surprising, then, that the Rough Riders felt
that they were next to plug the line while the Germans tried to turn the left
flank of the Allies. Entraining that night, the yeomen sincerely expected to end
up at Folkestone for the Channel crossing; in fact they were destined to guard
the east coast, at Norfolk.

---

18   Belgian refugees.
19   'Scheme', or 'stunt', meaning a large military exercise.
20   1st County of London Yeomanry (Middlesex Hussars), the senior regiment in the brigade.

What precipitated this move was the challenge by Admiral Hipper to the North Sea coast. Hipper, commander of the German battlecruiser squadron, was impatient. While the British Grand Fleet was operating as a coherent whole, based in the natural harbour of Scapa Flow in the Orkneys, the German High Seas Fleet was holed up in Wilhelmshaven. A German submarine had, however, scored a significant success in the English Channel on 22 September, when the U-9 had sunk the aging cruisers *Aboukir*, *Cressey* and *Hogue* with the loss of 1,450 sailors. If other British ships could be tempted out, it might be possible to destroy them piecemeal, thereby reducing the threat. Hipper spied an opportunity in raiding the east coast, and with the Kaiser forbidding a fleet action, such raids represented the only means of taking the fight to the British Navy.

On 2 November 1914, Admiral Hipper led his squadron with the cruisers SMS *Seydlitz*, *Von der Tann*, *Moltke* and *Blücher* and the light cruisers *Strassburg*, *Graudenz*, *Kolberg* and *Stralsund*. Aiming to lay mines, they were also to bombard the coastal town of Yarmouth. Arriving early morning the next day, just two elderly Royal Navy destroyers, HMS *Lively* and *Leopard*, and a minesweeper, HMS *Halcyon*, were all that stood in their way. Alerted to the danger, the British ships challenged the much greater German force and managed to draw fire before the enemy cruisers attempted a desultory bombardment of the coast – the shells landing harmlessly in the Norfolk sands. And before Admiral Beatty could despatch his more powerful force, Hipper's ships were making their way back to harbour.

Hipper was disappointed with the action, and the British rattled. It had demonstrated that the long east coast of England was a target – and that raids might just achieve the results that the German admiral hoped for, the reduction of the British naval force. Ripples of alarm spread through the country, and the yeomanry were despatched to the coast to repel all comers:

> An invasion scare took firm hold of the military and naval authorities. It was argued by the War Office that the lull on the fighting fronts would enable the Germans to spare large numbers of good troops – 250,000 if necessary – for the invasion of Great Britain. Lord Kitchener directed all defensive preparations to be made, and Lord Fisher threw himself into the task with gusto.[i]

The fear of invasion matched perfectly with the 'prediction' of William Le Queux's 1906 best-selling novel, *The Invasion of 1910*, which was commissioned by Alfred Harmsworth and serialised in the *Daily Mail*. The novel was born of the naval arms race that was then escalating between the two nations, and described the defeat of the British fleet in the North Sea by the German Navy, and the subsequent bombardment and invasion of the eastern counties:

Proclamation

Citizens of London

The news of the bombardment of the City of Newcastle and the landing of the German army at Hull, Weybourne, Yarmouth and other places along the East Coast is unfortunately confirmed.[ii]

Using such literary devices, the book seemed realistic and was extremely popular; its fictional outcome must have been playing in the minds of the public at least when the German Navy took to bombarding the east coast.

The whole of the 2nd Mounted Division were despatched to guard the coast, and to upgrade and install defences should the invader come. It was intended that the yeomen would provide both a mobile force at the coast that was capable of handling any emergency, backed up a stronger concentration of troops at nodal points inland. From Cromer south-eastwards for 10 miles, the Mounted Division spread out along the coast, the Rough Riders serving on the flank of the defences at Bacton-on-Sea. Here, the regiment set to work:

The first few days were passed in preparing defences. At Bacton, Walcott and Happisburgh Gaps, where roads led up from the beach, the existing trenches were enlarged and improved. Between the first two, as the cliff fell away to a mere bank, short lengths of fire-trench were dug. Elsewhere private stairways from the beach were demolished and wired. And inland, positions and emplacements were constructed at cross-roads and other commanding points.[iii]

Far from facing the Germans in Flanders, the Talley brothers were left with the prospect of tackling the winter on the exposed North Sea coast.

19 November 1914

Bacton, Norfolk

My darling Parents

Our Captain commandeered a nice little house for us,
the people by the name of Adcock who rent it were away at the
time we had to break in. Our stables are about $\frac{1}{4}$ mile away,
immediately opposite Bacton Church by a few little cottages,
I expect you will remember it I am enclosing a card.[21] Frank
is away from me, he is quite comfortable. I have a little bed
to lie on, one of these chair bedsteads which has warped in
places, but shall soon get use to it.

We consider ourselves at the front here under strict war
conditions. If you go on the beach at night you run the risk of
being shot at sight; we sleep with our rifles and 100 rounds by
our beds. I should like to tell you a few more secrets but dare
not. Mr Laurence, my Captain whose horse I look after, is a
nice chap.[22]

All our kit has been sent away to the base so we only have
what we stand up in which is most unfortunate only one pair of
boots, no clean underclothes but still, we are at war and must
put with such trifles. I should have liked to have told you
what we expected the other night down here but dare not, will
leave you to imagine.[23]

Ever your own son

Percy

---

21 The Talley family had evidently visited this part of Norfolk during the summer months.
22 Percy was acting as a groom; this relationship would sour.
23 In reference to one of many invasion scares on the Norfolk coast.

22 November 1914

My dear Mother

Percy has probably already told you that the parcel came along here from South Stoke and came in the nick of time, and as we had to go out to guard all night I took some of the cake and chocolate and was glad to have it. We started at 5 o'clock at night and came away about 6 in the morning. I was situated at the extreme right of our trenches and for shelter had to creep into a little bomb proof hole about 4ft wide and 5ft 9in-6ft long and just high enough to sit upright in. Unfortunately it was dug out in the sand, which kept falling. The wind was very high and blew the sand into our faces and stung us, and in spite of two blankets and my overcoat I had a job to keep warm. I might say that two of us had to sleep in the above mentioned small hole, so you can imagine how much room we had.

I had intended to ask you to send me down some clean things, although I have a complete change in my kit bag, this is about 7 miles away in the rear and we are not likely to see them again for some time. So if you could send down one of the thick shirts and a pair of pants I should be very glad to have them.

We had hoped to have had a quiet day today, but just as we were thinking of dinner we had instructions to saddle up with all our things on board, so we had to miss our dinner and get ready and then go into the trenches for about an hour. All this was done on information and instruction from the War Office, so it seems likely that the Germans may try and invade us, but I guess we are ready if they do come, which I now very much doubt, should such a thing occur we will wire as often as possible how we are or if we cannot will send postcard, but don't worry about that it is not likely to happen.

Ever your loving son

Frank

23 November 1914

My dear Parents

  Tonight here is very critical. We are expecting to be raided,
every man of our troop is on guard on the beach. I am on guard
at our house to our stables about 300 yds or more all alone,
the nearest place to communicate is Eden Hall. The roads as you
know are very lonely and dark, the evening is clearing. I am
pleased to say it started very bad and was most depressing.
I have to go out about every hour. I started guard about 5 pm,
it goes on all night, no relief, so I guess I shall be pretty
tired. I have just put a clip of 5 rounds in my rifle. I do not
intend to run any risks. The H.A.C.[24] have come in, I should think
only for the night, and they have brought their guns, so think
we shall make a fairly good show if anything happens. The place
seems to be full up with spies, arrests have been made and
numerous people chased. Personally I think it is absurd to
leave one man on my job but there you are, I am told to do it so
I must, our horses are all saddled, and have to remain so all
night. I received your letter this afternoon. Am afraid this
letter is a bit of a jumble but you know the circumstances I am
writing under, shall have to be going out again soon.

  Ever your own son

Percy

(With the movement of the trees caused by the strong wind
I think somebody is coming, I am getting used to it now.
The civilians are very nervy, they do not know what to say
when you challenge and they see your bayonet.)

---

24 Honourable Artillery Company: A and B Batteries were attached to the 4th London
    Mounted Brigade, providing artillery support.

25 November 1914

My dear Parents

Your letter I read this morning, it is very good of you to send me the watch. This morning we turned out, as we had an alarm; the result was we had our breakfast at 1 pm, now it is 5 and we have to go on our night vigil on the cliffs. The clean clothes will be a godsend I will do as you say and send others home. Will you please send my brown boots. I think you know them, rather a vivid colour. I must be off now, will acknowledge parcel.

Ever your own son

Percy

(I am so worried to give you so much trouble with sending things.)

29 November 1914

My dear Father

Percy has perhaps written and told you that he had gone to
one of our other squadrons (B) as one officer whose horse he
looks after has been transferred. He could have given up the
job, I think and stayed on with us, but the officer particularly asked him to stay on. As he has treated him well up to
the present, he decided to do so, it may be well to keep in
with him as he is a stock exchange man and may be able to do
him a good turn.

Please thank mother for the sponge and tobacco, both are
very welcome. Tonight I have to go on duty on the coast, this
I believe is one thing Percy will miss, as his squadron have
not done any of the work yet.

Only another four weeks to Xmas, I am afraid we shall not be
home for it this year, and it will certainly be the quietest
we have spent, there has been a rumour going round that we
shall get 48 hours leave but shall not believe it until then.
Something more definite of course we cannot all leave at the
same time, so it will have to be done in shifts.

Ever your affectionate son

Frank

30 November 1914

3 Troop
B Squadron
Battle Court
Bacton
Nth Walsham
Norfolk
On Service

My darling Parents

The tobacco and pipe came this morning quite safely, later
the sponge parcel came but no boots, presume they are coming by
another post, thank you so much for the tobacco and toffee. You
will see by the address that I have shifted, my officer has gone
to B Squadron so of course he wanted me to go. I said I wouldn't
at first, but said I would, after; he was very pleased. I am
just as near Frank at present while we are here. This new billet
I am at, we have a bath and lavatories and wash basins combined,
of course I lose my feather bed which I was very sick about,
but I told Mr Laurence I have not been well for the last three
weeks and he has worked it that I sleep on the couch in the
smoking room, which will not be so bad, think it will pay me to
keep in with him. We all pay 2/6 a week for mess, which includes
such things was porridge for breakfast and sweets for dinner,
and there is plenty of room to sit down for all in the dining
room. I do hope the boots will turn up alright when I sent these
home. Think I had better have a few nails put round the heel
and toes. The weather has been very wet and miserable water all
over the roads. Today is Sunday and we heard we had to do trench
digging but our Captain has got us off.

Ever your loving son

39

3 December 1914

My dear Mother

Today again has been glorious although a bit cold and tonight is certainly much more so. It is really our turn for night duty, but that has been stopped anyhow for the present, I believe they have got more of the infantry Territorials down for the job which I think is only right as they do not appear to do any work during the day, while we are out at all times.

Yesterday we were out on the sands for troop drill and then Regimental Drill under the Colonel with drawn swords at the Gallop. It was rather heavy going for the horses and tiring for us, as the sand was very loose in some parts. We had to wade through the water up to the horse's breast, but of course the salt water is very good for them.

It is getting late now and I want to give my rifle a clean up, so will stop.

Ever your affectionate son

Frank

6 December 1914

My dear Mother

I expect you will be pleased to hear that our leave has been
extended to one week, as yet we do not know when our turn comes but
probably within the next week or two, it will be very nice to get
home again and after our present time will seem quite a long holiday.

Yesterday, here was a glorious day but very cold but I don't
seem to feel it very much except about the ears. I think as
regards weather we are getting pretty well hardened.

We have been rubbing castor oil in our saddles and bri-
dles, etc., to preserve it, this is also very good for boots,
if you have any that are hard or let the wet in I think you
will find it a good tip, I have put some on mine and they are
certainly more soft and pliable.

This is my last piece of notepaper until tomorrow when I can
buy some more.

Your affectionate son

Frank

7 December 1914

My darling Parents

Just a line to tell you leave is official, I start on the 27th
for 7 days returning on 4th Jan. As regards a parcel for Xmas
I think it would be rather nice, it would be better if you sent
one to each of us as it is so awkward to split with Frank not
being in the same billet of course. Frank may be home for Xmas,
I must write you later. Today is Sunday and we have had a quiet
day, it is much colder this morning there was a heavy frost. I am
keeping fit in spite of all. I feel quite different knowing that
I shall be home so soon for such a long stay. I must close now
dinner is nearly ready.

Ever your own son

Percy

13 December 1914

My dear Mother

I am afraid I have no news to give you just now, except to report on the weather, which yesterday and today has been awful incessant rain the whole time.

I think it is now pretty certain that we shall get five days leave, but when we cannot yet say, but I should think it most likely to be over by the end of this year.

On Friday we had dummy thrusting.[25] It was not quite up to the Military Tournament standard, my horse went all right up to the hanging dummies, but shied at those on the ground so that I could not get any where near them, but on the whole our Sergeant Major said it was not bad.

I am sorry this is a short letter but news is absolutely nil, and you know the place well enough to know that there is nothing to do at night time.

Your affectionate son

Frank

---

25   Sword practice; the British cavalry pattern sword was designed for thrusting in the charge rather than slashing like a sabre.

16 December 1914

My darling Parents

   The other day we had a cavalry charge. I suppose there was
about 100 of us in line; we broke into a quiet gallop, then
our Captain gave the order to charge. We simply went for it,
of course this was with drawn swords, it was most thrilling.
   I have been trying to have a sleep before tea but the floor
is oh so hard, today I feel so tired and weary, my muscles
are so hard and developed that it feels if they would burst
if I had to use my arms much more. Yesterday we had a scheme,
it started to rain so the order came along to put on our coats.
As soon as we had done this it cleared up and was quite warm,
but still we had to keep them on until we had finished. What
with having to dismount with our rifles, run along, climb
banks and throw ourselves down, fire and up again, then up
and mount and off again, it was truly terrible. For two pins,
I would have stopped and lay down in the road, it would make
such a difference if the enemy were Germans.[26] If I am lucky to
have seven days leave think I must spend the final day in bed.
   Ever your loving son

   Per

---

26   In this case, the 'enemy' was another troop of yeomen, taking part in a 'scheme',
     or training exercise.

17 December 1914

My dear Mother

    Tuesday evening, I had a telegram from the Sergeant Major whose horse I look after to saddle up and meet him at North Walsham[27] at 8.43. This meant, of course, saddling his and mine own horse and leading his all the way. It took past an hour to get there, the night was awfully dark, but fortunately I had the telegraph posts for a guide, although I could barely see from one post to another. However, I managed to get there in safety and also back, Percy had to do it last night for his officer. He is back alright as I just caught a glimpse of him on parade this morning.

    I should be glad if you could send along a clean shirt and a pair of pants, the ones I leave off I will get washed down here, I have already had some socks done. It is getting on now so I must go and feed my horses.

Your affectionate son

Frank

Admiral Hipper's first attempt at a raid off the North Sea coast in early November had aimed to draw British ships away from the Grand Fleet, thereby enabling the Germans to pick off their enemy one by one. This action had highlighted the vulnerability of East Anglia to German raids, and had led directly to the 2nd Mounted Division being actively deployed in the defence of the homeland.

On 14 December, the British Admiralty deciphered messages that indicated that the German battlecruiser squadron was once again going to make an attempt on the coast of England. Controversially, Admiral Beatty made the assessment that if the Royal Navy could destroy the German squadron, then the whole German Imperial High Seas Fleet would be severely weakened. But this would come at a cost; the German ships would be allowed to make their attack, and then be taken on the return leg by the Royal Navy.

---

27   4½ miles inland from Bacton.

At 8 a.m. on 16 December, SMS *Derflinger* and *Von der Tann* started bombarding the coastal resort of Scarborough, the *Seydlitz*, *Blücher* and *Moltke* attacking Hartlepool. As Winston Churchill was to write: 'the great shells crashed into the little houses of Hartlepool and Scarborough, carrying their cruel messages of pain and anxiety.'[iv] The raid killed some 137 civilians, and caused 592 casualties. And when the German ships were able to escape into the mists and poor visibility of the North Sea, the Admiralty had missed its chance.

For the Talley brothers, based on the east coast, the attack served as a reminder of the vulnerability of the coast and led to further invasion scares, such as that which took place on 23 December, effectively interrupting Christmas. There was no truce here on the bitingly cold North Sea coast.

18 December 1914

My darling Parents

The morning the Germans bombarded Scarboro, we were called up at 4.30 in the morning and had to stand by our horses already saddled until 8.30, when another troop took over the duty.

Yesterday we had to take our horses out bare back. We tried to make them jump, but the jump we erected had no sides, which made it difficult to make them go over. We also had to dismount at the gallop, of course bare back it is really not so difficult as it looks. Today has been beautiful cold but bright; we were inspected on the beach, this was quite a joy ride as we simply rode to a point 5 miles away and came back.

Ever your loving son

20 December 1914

My dear Mother
  The Scarboro and Hartlepool affair seems to have been worse than was first imagined, but so far it has not made any difference to us; the H.A.C.[28] who are down here, are going to do some firing tomorrow and the people have or are to be warned to keep indoors.
  Your affectionate son

  Frank

23 December 1914

Leave suddenly stopped, cannot give any particulars.[29] If any other changes and I can get away expect me when you see me.
  In haste, yours

  Frank

---

28 A and B Batteries, Honourable Artillery Company, provided horse artillery support for the London Mounted Brigade, and if threatened from the sea, could have returned fire.

29 A.S. Hamilton described the alarm in 1936: 'a fresh invasion scare caused all leave to be stopped; those who had actually set out were turned back from North Walsham Station. Everyone slept fully dressed that night and stood to arms at his alarm post next morning from 4.a.m till daylight. The same procedure was repeated the next night, so that the Regiment spent part of its Christmas in the trenches.'

23 December 1914

My dear Parents

Today has been simply grand a heavy frost in the night, which
has been about all day, but the sun has been out which has made
it truly good. I do not think you need worry about me. I feel
quite fit except for my toes when I take my socks off, and my
bad nights, but I am quite used to not having much sleep by now,
except sometimes it plays me up. We went out for bare back riding
again. I came off a bad smack while galloping, but no harm done
after when jumping. I got over the jump quite safely, but my
pony, when he cleared, threw his head forward and I went right
over his head. Still no harm done except a nasty shakening.

24 December 1914

My dear Mother

Please excuse a short and hurried line, but I want to get this
off my hands in case anything happens[30] and we have to clear out.
As my card of yesterday will have told you, all leave has been
stopped, anyhow for the present. We only got the news yesterday
about 12.30 after returning from an early morning inspection by the
Brigadier, some fellows who had got into a trap to go to the station,
and two officers who went the day before, have been recalled.
Many thanks for the parcel which only reached me today, everything in it looks very nice, especially the pudding which I am
sure will be up to the usual quality, I was very glad to have
the pants and have posted the dirty pair and also the shirt. You
will find the pants in a very bad state and if you think it not
worth mending, they will do for patching.
Ever your affectionate son

Frank

---

30 Referring to the continued invasion scare.

25 December 1914

My darling Parents

The parcel was simply grand. The only thing was we were
warned that evening that we should have to rise at 3 o'clock in
the morning, as we were expecting the Germans to raid the East
Coast. So we were warned we might not return to our billet,
so the result was I had one quarter of the pudding, and gave
the other piece and cake and grapes away, but I kept the dates
raisins, etc., to myself.

We are still here and tomorrow will be the third morning we
shall have to rise at 3. It is very weird and so cold. If we
get no more alarms, leave I think starts on Tuesday, so Frank
will be home, with good luck I should leave Sunday week. We all
at 6 o'clock go off for our Xmas dinner at some big place.
I forgot to sign the card I sent. The cigarettes were simply
grand. Today has been terrible cold, freezing hard as the day
advances. I do hope you will all have a happy time I have been
thinking of you all the whole time.

Ever your own son

49

27 December 1914

My dear Mother

It has been our strangest Christmas, Friday morning we were
in the trenches from 5.30 until after 10. It was a glorious day,
but very cold. It was rather misty, and we could only just see
the sun from the cliffs, so had to stay there longer than we
otherwise would have done.

Owing to the alarm we have not had much work to do during the
day, but have to keep fairly near our horses in case of alarm
and while in the trenches in the morning we leave them fully
saddled, so if the necessity arose the whole squadron could
move off within a few minutes. I think the authorities thought
that the Germans might possibly try to make a landing during
the holidays, as they know what sort of time we have and that
a lot of the fellows would be away on leave. However, nothing
has happened and are still fit and well, but as regards leave
being resumed we have heard nothing so far, although hoping
that we shall get away.

Ever your affectionate son

Frank

29 December 1914

My darling Parents

I received your letter this morning quite safely. We have
moved again, it is rotten, not a patch on our other place.
Miserable stables, well I won't say anymore about it, I feel
so miserable, they seem to be playing the fool with us. I hope
to be home in about a week's time with any luck so do not worry
about any clean clothes. I am getting quite used to my dirty
pants and shirt by now. Last night was terrible, the wind and
rain, this place we are at simply rocked. I thought it would
come down about our ears, water comes in the kitchen. I suppose
Frank is home by now I heard his squadron had left.[31]

Xmas day we had our dinner in the evening, also on Boxing Day
we had another when the Captain of the Squadron came we had a
real good feed. This place is about 2 miles away from our old
billet, Ridlington by name I expect you know it, near Walcott.
So think if you substitute this Ridlington in place of Bacton
I ought to receive letters, as they all go to headquarters.
I do hope you all had a happy Xmas I have been wondering what
you were doing.

Ever your own son

Percy

---

31 Percy was still in B Squadron; Frank in D.

30 December 1914

My dear Mother

There is not very much news to give you, I have just about got to the end of your parcel and can only say that it has all been very good and much appreciated. I am glad to say that leave has again been resumed and hope to be one of the next lot to go, which will probably be Saturday or Monday.

Percy's Squadron I expect you have heard, have moved to a place nearer the cliffs and it has brought him a little nearer to me, I have not found out yet where he is, but he may look me up first to tell me.

It is quite possible as I did not get my leave last Monday when it was resumed that we may be home together after all but this is a very uncertain sort of life and we never know what is going to happen.

I hope you are all keeping fit in spite of the bad weather and fogs you have been having. I felt like a cold yesterday but took some quinine[32] and feel quite OK today.

Your affectionate son

Frank

---

32 A traditional fever-reducing medicine derived from the bark of tropical trees, commonly associated with the treatment of malaria.

1 January 1915

> B Squadron Headquarters
> Rough Riders
> City of Ldn Yeomanry
> Bacton
> Norfolk

My dear Parents

You will see by the address that I have another move, our headquarters were such a distance from my officer that he has made arrangements for me to be nearer, so I am just behind the officers house in a little place and I must say I am very much more comfortable. I went round and borrowed a mattress so I have good nights. I am quite near Frank again.

We had drill on the beach today bare back, I shall soon be able to ride as well without the saddle as with it. It is now blowing a gale and raining. This morning was grand, roads very slippery and now rain and wind. Well I will tell you all news and incidents when I come home. I had my first hot bath since I was last home (keep it dark). My word, the mud in spite of doing my best to keep clean, as you know.

Ever your own son

Percy

6 January 1915

My dear Parents

As Frank is now home I hope he will tell you of all our doings. I tried hard to come today but could not but think for certain I shall be home on the 15th we have a very big inspection on the 14th and nobody will be allowed to go till after it is over. I feel absolutely disheartened and so miserable I could either cry or fight somebody but suppose I must put up with it. We are having such wet weather but I seem to keep fit in spite of it all, some of the fellows have terrible coughs and throats. I feel too miserable to write any more so will say goodbye with all my best love to you all.

Ever your own son

Per

10 January 1915

Returned safely comfortable journey down about 15 minutes late. It has been fine and cold up to 5 o'clock since then has been raining hard. Have been busy all day cleaning up stirrups bridle and buckles, etc., for Wednesday inspection.

Yours

Frank

17 January 1915

My dear Mother

No news is good news, at least I hope so, as I have not heard from you since I came back, perhaps the letters have gone over to 'B' Squadron by mistake.

I have had a very bad cold and throat during this last week Wednesday and Thursday it being pretty bad, fortunately it has not gone to my chest probably because of the quinine I took. We continue to have our daily quota of rain which just lays the dust although during the night and then morning we had a little snow for variation, just at present it is cold and fine.

Percy I suppose got home on Thursday, he will have given you all news and rumours. I think it is generally believed that we shall not go to France at all, whether we shall get as far as Egypt or not I don't know. I think I told you what one of our fellows heard as the opinion of General French's staff[33] and the war being over in March. It is now 12.30 so I must get my horses watered and fed.

Ever your affectionate son

Frank

The German naval attacks on the east coast were by no means restricted to bombardment by cruisers, for now the history of warfare entered a new phase with the use of naval Zeppelin attacks over the mainland of Britain. On 19 January 1915, two airships set out to attack the industrial centres of the north-east coast. They were equipped with enough fuel for thirty hours of continuous flight, and each carried with them eight bombs and twenty-five incendiary devices, consisting of kerosene-filled containers wrapped in tar-covered rope. It was fortunate that these primitive devices were largely ineffective.

---

33   Field Marshal Sir John French was commander-in-chief of the British Expeditionary Force in France and Flanders.

Poor weather meant that these aviation pioneers had no hope of reaching Humberside, and as such, the coastal towns of Norfolk, including the seaside resort of Great Yarmouth – on the coast just to the south of that stretch occupied by the men of the 2nd Mounted Division – became their unlikely targets. Zeppelin L4 was the first aircraft to drop a bomb on British soil, at Sheringham, 16 miles to the north-west of Bacton; Zeppelin L3 was first to kill a British civilian, 24 miles to the south-east, in Great Yarmouth. The raid caused great consternation amongst civilians – and scare stories of spies and sympathisers signalling to the enemy were rife. There was much more to come.

20 January 1915

My dear Father

Percy has just been over to see me for a few minutes, I could not go myself to him as since Sunday I have had a rather bad attack of rheumatism in my left ankle and have hardly been able to put my foot to the ground. I managed to borrow some horse liniment from one of the fellows yesterday containing a large proportion of turps; whether it was that or not I don't know, but I am glad to say that it is practically alright today.

You will of course have read of the airship raid yesterday some of our fellows actually saw them, but did not know that they were German otherwise they would have had a shot at them, fortunately the loss of life and damage was very small.

I understand from Percy that you have a pair of putties from Walter[34] for me. I should be very glad if you would send them down as my present pair are nearly in halves in several places and therefore very untidy.

Ever your affectionate son

Frank

---

34   Walter was an older brother.

23 January 1915

My darling Parents,

I was so pleased to receive your letter, it quite bucked
me up. Today has been quite fine a heavy frost in the morning. I have been picked for a football team, our colours are
white nickers, blue socks with light blue (sky) round the tops,
shirts heliotrope[35] with skyblue neck band, and done up in
front with skyblue lace so guess we shall look quite smart. Has
anyone from the office acknowledged my photos yet. Some of our
fellows saw the light of the German airships, it does not seem
to worry us greatly. I have had such bad nights the pillow is
not comfortable, so today I have got an old sack and filled it
with hay and hope to sleep better.

Ever your loving son

Per

24 January 1915

My dear Mother

Percy's late officer he tells me is going back to the base
(presumably because he is no good) and after chucking him they
now tell him he is to go back with him, of course he does not
want to and I have told him to see his Major although this is
not the correct thing to do, anyhow I don't think he need worry
as I believe if he does not wish to take up the job again they
cannot compel him to. Now I must write a line to Walter to
thank him for the chocolate and putties.

Ever your affectionate son

Frank

---

35 Heliotrope is a pink-purple shade, named after a flower. Sports, and particularly
football, were extremely important in building and maintaining morale and team spirit.

24 January 1915

My darling Parents,

I arrived safely with a crowded carriage although pleasant.[36]
The soldier you saw in the corner had just come out of hospital
and was ill. He had been wounded in both legs by shrapnel,
he showed us the wounds in one leg, it was terrible, he was a
regular soldier but quite smart; he can make himself understood in five languages. I must say I had a more comfortable
night with my pillow, but I do feel so miserable, it is terrible. It is pouring with rain and mud as well. I am on guard
tonight so I am asking one of them here to post this for me so
hope you will receive it safely, of course I cannot go and see
Frank yet, things are just the same here some of our fellows
saw the German airships last night. This is only a note to tell
you I arrived safely.

Ever your loving son

Percy

36   Percy was returning from a period of leave, now granted after the invasion scares
      of December.

27 January 1915

My darling Parents

This just a note to say I am going back to D Squadron, so think you had better address all my letters there. At the present I am at Happisburgh about 3 miles from Bacton.[37] My man has been sent here and although I have had nothing to do with him for some time now I had to go because I came with him which is very unjust so? I told him so and said I would not go. He threatened to have me arrested, so I went direct to my old major and he said he would be very pleased to have me back. I will not write you anymore details now but I have been very upset and not feeling fit, but I hope things will soon be alright I might possibly go back to D tonight.

Ever your own son

Pex

---

37   Towards Great Yarmouth. Percy was still acting as an officer's groom, but was clearly having some problems, and hoped to return to D Squadron.

28 January 1915

My dear Mother

Many thanks for your last letter enclosed with the putties. Percy has had to go to the base with Laurence, but I believe he will be coming back to this Squadron he saw our Major and he consented to have him back and I hope he will be over this week.

Did I tell you that I had been turned out of my billet, as they have taken the place for a store room, so I am now sleeping at Edenhall[38] in a very comfortable spring bed, it is a very nice change and I am making the most of it, it is a treat to get in between clean sheets again.

I have heard a rumour that we are moving on the 10th of next month but how true it is, it is impossible to say any how for the present, but I will let you know anything definite that I hear.

Ever your affectionate son

Frank

---

38 A large house at Bacton that was later to be used as a school for 'sick and delicate children'.

The pressures of service were starting to tell on Percy Talley. Acting as a groom for his officer, Captain Laurence, he had been transferred to B Squadron, away from his brother. What actually happened is difficult to discern, but it is likely that Laurence was something of a martinet, and Percy, an educated man who worked in the City of London, was less than happy to take direction. Disobeying an order from a superior officer, or going so far as striking an officer, was a serious insubordination according to the Army Act 1913, Part 1:

> Every person subject to military law who commits any of the following offences; that is to say ... being concerned in any quarrel, fray or disorder, refuses to obey any officer ... who orders him into arrest, or strikes, or uses or offers violence to, any such officer ... shall on conviction by court-marshal be liable ... to suffer imprisonment.[v]

The realities of service must have been trying to many men, who realised they were under the complete control of the army. If Percy had struck his officer, he would have been liable, if proven guilty, to at least 112 days' detention.[39]

---

39 *The King's Regulations and Orders for the Army 1912* (Reprinted 1914), p.133.

29 January 1915

My darling Parents

    I am afraid my last letter will have put a damper on the other which seemed to cheer you up. He[40] came to me last Sunday morning and told me I should have to go with him, of course he could see I did not like it and I told him so. He said it was in orders, so I went to the Captain. He was nice enough but said I must go, I was advised by my - name I will not mention - that in King's Regulation I need to do so. He said to me I ought to go back and say I do not wish to do it. I did, with the result that he Laurence said he would have me arrested if I was not ready in the morning. On that I went straight to my old Major, and he said he would be pleased to have me back. I went back again to tell them this but no avail I had to go and on the way in the morning he was very angry and shouted at me so I thought the best thing to do was to answer him back which seemed to sober him a little, and few hours after our arrival he said he had signed my transfer.

    I think you had better address my letters to D Squadron. I may not get them for a time and yet I might if I went back tomorrow. I shall write Frank that you are doing so. I can tell you it was as much as I could do to keep my hands off him but I did. I am glad today. This business has nearly finished me, it is as much as I can do to bear up, you must not let it worry you but it does relieve one to tell somebody and after all you are the ones to tell.

    Ever your loving son

Per

1 pair putties, shirt and socks have been issued so do not send anything.

---

40   Percy's officer, Laurence.

31 January 1915

My dear Mother

I believe our Belgian friends go on Tuesday, what part of
France are they going to? Please give them my love.[41] News is
absolutely scarce with us, I have heard no more about the
rumour[42] but will let you know anything that comes along.

Ever your affectionate son

Frank

31 January 1915

My darling Parents

This is Sunday morning and a terribly miserable one too, raining very blooming hard. I hired a bike and rode over to see Frank
and one or two of them and they said things were going alright
and ought to be back soon to D.[43] Think you had better address to
D and I must take my chance when I receive them, I will write you
as often as possible. How are you all keeping? I trust fit and
well of course. You are worried about me but cheer up and I will
try and do the same I almost regret having told you but it eased
my mind so much as I was very nearly doing something desperate.[44]

I think you had better bank my pay this month. I am spending
such a lot on food here as the stuff is awful. I go to a little
place and have tea everyday which costs me with two eggs 1/3,
without 1/-, I have done this already about four times and am
doing so again today.

Ever your loving son

Percy

---

41 The Talley family had played host to six Belgian refugees from the early part of the war.
42 The rumour that the City of London Yeomanry were being sent to Egypt.
43 D Squadron.
44 It seems that Percy was close to striking his officer, a serious offence.

3 February 1915

My darling Parents

You will be pleased to hear that my transfer has been put
through, I was to have gone back tonight, but I was not keen
on going tonight with all my kit which I should have to carry
down to headquarters, which is a quarter of an hour's walk and
would have meant three journeys, and travelling with officers,
and then the chance of there not being room, so I hope to go
tomorrow Thursday. Whether I go to my old troop I cannot say
but think I shall.

Ever your loving son

Percy

5 February 1915

My dear Father

Thanks for your letter of the 2nd I only received it last night,
though I should have had it before, but it was lying at the troop
billet and I did not get time until after tea to go for it.

I don't think anything in it requires special reference,
except about Percy, as I told you in my last letter our Major
was agreeable to having him back in the old Squadron, and yesterday he turned up with all his kit and is now with us again
and so hope his trouble in this direction are finished with.

There is nothing fresh to give you in the way of news and
I shall be off in a minute or two for sword exercise which we
are now getting nearly every day so I must close now.

Ever your affectionate son

Frank

5 February 1915

My darling Parents

Your letter of yesterday I have just received. I came over to
D Squadron on Thursday. Everybody has been most kind, all the
fellows shook hands with me, and I feel quite happy. Our troop
is in two billets, I am in one past Webster's the post office
on the left hand side, ten of us are here and we are quite
comfortable. I was really beginning to feel quite ill, getting
weak and weary but now I have bucked up and begin to feel my
old self again, muscles getting hard, etc. Of course I have
no horse and no equipment, but think with a little luck I may
have quite a nice little horse which I have my eye on, and the
sergeant has promised to help me.

Ever your loving son

Percy

9 February 1915

My dear Mother

Today has been rotten with plenty of rain; we were out in it
all this morning galloping about in a very muddy field and
trying to make our horses jump the hedges, but I was not very
successful as my old beast is not very sure footed and I have
quite enough work to do to keep him up. I have managed to
make him answer the proper rein and makes it very much easier
for drilling, though I wanted it chiefly for dummy thrusting,
which we have not had lately.

Ever your affectionate son

Frank

9 February 1915

My darling Parents
    Thank you so much for the 5/- you sent, it was most acceptable as I was running short. I am quite happy, in spite of the awful weather we are having mud up to your eyes. Have you heard from Marguerite yet, if they have arrived safely?[45] I am quite busy what with trying to procure my new kit.[46] I was on guard Sunday 6.30 (night) till Monday 6.30 pm so have not had over much time for writing.
    Ever your loving son

Percy

---

45   Marguerite was one of the Belgian refugees who had been staying with the Talley family, and who had moved to France.
46   Having moved squadrons, from B back to D, Percy had to have some major items of his equipment, which remained on the squadron manifest, reissued – rifle, sword, and so on.

10 February 1915

My dear Parents

Thank you for sending the pants I received them last night,
it was quite comforting to get into them I soon shall be sending
one or two dirty things which you might keep until I want them.
I shall then have two shirts with me. I have been cook this week,
I do not like the job – at least I don't mind the cooking but
the washing up ... My menu? We are ten here, for lunch was Welsh
rarebit, roast beef, potatoes, carrots and onions, rice pudding
and prunes, which I cooked myself. They like my rice pudding
very much, I shall soon be quite an expert. Of course the cook
does not turn out for parades, unless for a special one; well we
have had two this week so you see I have had my hands full. You
do not get finished much before 6.30-7 o'clock sometimes if you
are smart you can have one hour in the afternoon. I also have to
sweep and tidy the dining room and light the fire. For breakfast
we have fried bacon and bread in the fat.

Ever your loving son

Percy

11 February 1915

Many thanks for your letter last night. Percy's also came by
the same post, as we are again together in the same troop it
may save you time if you are in a hurry to write only to one of
us as we can now get the news from one another.

Ever your affectionate son

Frank

11 February 1915

My darling Parents

I received your letter last night think you might send me a pair of pants. As regards my equipment, of course when you go to a different squadron you have to hand in everything to the old squadron, and receive somebody else's when you go to the new one, of course this applies to rifle, sword, bayonet, etc. I have not a horse of my own, but that will come in time as we are going to have new ones. The Major spoke to me on parade today asking me if I was pleased to be back. I said yes, rather. The cottage I am staying at is called May Cottage so think you might add that to the address to make sure I get things quicker. I am keeping fit although there is a lot of illness here, we have a sick billet now which is pretty full.

Ever your loving son

Percy

It was essential to maintain fitness and to prepare the Rough Riders for whatever trials they were going to face in the months ahead. With the whole of the 2nd Mounted Division deployed to the coast of Norfolk, training, active sports and exercises continued as the threat of invasion subsided:

> During the first two months of 1915 troop and squadron training was first carried out, with mounted parades five mornings a week and dismounted arms drill two or three afternoons, but the routine was varied by regimental days, brigade schemes, bad weather and scares. Men, horses, billets and stables were periodically inspected by various Brigade and Divisional officers, but none so searchingly than General Peyton ... Saturdays were spent in fatigues and cleaning up, and on Sundays squadrons attended service at their parish churches.[vi]

17 February 1915

My dear Mother

Yesterday we had a rather long scheme[47] on, starting at 7.46 and getting back after 2 o'clock, doing in all about 22 miles. Our squadron did not have much work to do as we were held in reserve, fortunately it was a glorious day on the whole quite warm, just the opposite to today, until about 6 o'clock. I don't think it has left off raining the whole day.

Tonight one of the Middlesex Yeomanry[48] squadrons are having a concert at Edenhall. They have got a good platform and decorations up and the place looks quite smart, the second half I believe is to be a minstrel business, one of their Captains is leader and I think it will be a very good affair, the men are just beginning to come in now, so I had better stop.

Ever your affectionate son

Frank

---

47 A 'scheme' was an exercise.

48 The senior yeomanry regiment in the Brigade, the 1st County of London Yeomanry (Middlesex Hussars).

19 February 1915

My darling Parents

My job as cook I am thankful to say is nearly at an end, they have been quite pleased with me, the stew today they said was fine nice gravy, not fatty. In the stew I put carrots, onions and potatoes, I also made a rice pudding, stewed rhubarb and also a jam roll, they were very pleased. When I come home you will have to let me cook for you. As regards the cooking we have to do a week each man. My equipment I have, but no horse and I am not the only one, we sent two away last week so we expect to have others in their place.

Ever your loving son

Percy

21 February 1915

My darling Parents

I have nothing more to report I am still expecting everyday to be moved to D, but still feel very depressed. Things go on just the same. Will now say goodbye as I am off to the village to have some tea.

Ever your loving son

Percy

22 February 1915

My dear Father

The weather for the last three days has been quite good especially yesterday it was gloriously fine and warm. Today we had
a big scheme on, and were away from here at 8.15 and not back
until 1.45. We had quite an exciting morning and think the
honours lie with us as the Sharp Shooters[49] were up against us.

My old horse on Saturday went lame and I had to bring her
back. I knew she had corns on her front hoofs[50] and when the
shoes were taken off and the hoof cut down it was found to be
quilin, which is a very bad form of corn. The Vet[51] tells me
tonight that he will probably have to cast it as unsurvivable.
Today I had to borrow another horse, which had not been out for
nearly a week, and consequently was very lively, but I got on
quite well, though once it tried to bolt with me.

Affectionate son

Frank

---

49 3rd County of London Yeomanry (Sharp Shooters), the third regiment in the London
    Mounted Brigade.
50 Corns in horses are specific bruises of the sole of the hoof close to its wall; they are
    formed by inadequately fitted shoes, or wedged stones, and are very painful for the horse.
51 Each division had veterinary support from personnel in the Army Veterinary Corps. At the
    outbreak of war, Mobile Veterinary Sections (MVS) were formed, and these accompanied
    the fighting divisions overseas. Captain Reginald C. Matthews was the Rough Riders' vet.

23 February 1915

My darling Parents

  I am glad to say I am quite fit and well, and have now a horse, it is a beauty a chestnut – goes like the wind and has plenty of spirit. It was a horse we had at South Stoke some months back, but it was very ill with strangles[52] and the trooper who has been riding it is too heavy the vet says. He said I was about the right weight for the horse, so my Sergeant has given it to me. Today has been grand. This morning we were out for drill and this horse I was riding led every time in the charges; it has a very strong mouth, but I am very pleased. I had a letter from Marguerite and a note on it from Lily, they seem to be very comfortable and having a good time although quiet, Marguerite seems very grateful for all you have done for them. It is now nearly 4 o'clock and we have to go to stables and I am on Main Guard tonight 6.50 till tomorrow 6.30, so you see I have not much time.

  Ever your loving son

Percy

---

52 'Strangles' is a common and extremely infectious equine respiratory disease that is a major threat to horse populations; this would have been a significant worry for the veterinary surgeons.

25 February 1915

My darling Parents

I received your letter on Monday. Today has been hard work
although enjoyable we had a scheme, leaving 9.30 returning
3 o'clock I have done quite a lot of riding, being sent out to
discover the enemy and find out how the land lies. This means,
of course, riding over the same ground time and again but it
is good sport not knowing whether you are going to be captured.
You may be riding quietly along then in the distance or around
the bend in the road you suddenly come upon the enemy (we go
out in sections of four men), which may be one or two men or a
whole troop. In the later case you have to turn round and fly
for your life and report to the officer, sometimes we see two
or three of them coming who have been sent out to see that all
is clear. If we spot them we lie in wait and capture them.

It is still very muddy about here the last two mornings we
have had heavy frosts, but the sun soon comes out and turns it
all to slush, some fields we come over today were in a terrible condition our horses were covered, which makes hard work
getting it off. Last night we had a concert to present Major
Clark[53] with a silver cigar box with an inscription; he has left
D Squadron and is now second in Command of the whole regiment,
and think before long he will be made Colonel of the regiment
which means Supreme Command. Well, think I have given you all
the news. I am quite fit, we have in our squadron about ¼ of
the men on the sick list so suppose I am lucky.

Ever your loving son

Percy

---

53   Major Goland Clarke was a veteran of the Boer War, having served with the 18th Hussars.
He was an active field naturalist. Resigning his commission as a captain in 1907,
he joined the Rough Riders and was promoted to major. He went on to command the
Rough Riders and survive the war; Percy's prediction was proven correct.

26 February 1915

My dear Mother

I think I told you in my last letter that there was a rumour,
which originated with the Middlesex Yeomanry, that we were
going over to France on the 10th of next month, this I am
almost sure is wrong, as unless we were sent off in a hurry we
should probably have 48 hours leave, and I believe they have
fixed the 27th for our regimental sports, so it looks rather
the other way, and we may be here for some time.

We had a concert on Wednesday night chiefly in order to make a
presentation to Major Clark our late head, it was a silver cigar
box with an inscription and also a reproduction of the badge
which we wear in our caps together with about 300 cigars, he was
of course told why he was wanted at the concert and think he was
surprised to hear about it and certainly appreciated it.

I think I mentioned in my last letter that my horse had gone
lame, due to very bad corns in both front feet. I had rather
hoped to have got it cast, as it stumbles rather frequently,
but don't think the Vet will do so, the corns have been cut out,
so it may make it better at present it is in the sick lines.

Your affectionate son

Frank

In February 1915, the opening shots of the Gallipoli Campaign, designed to knock the Ottoman Turks out of the war by naval force, were fired. From its inception, the campaign was intended to be a naval one, with a coalition of British, French and even Russian ships forcing their way through the narrow passage of the Dardanelles, the seaway that marks the boundary between the European and Asian continents. The principle was a simple one: if the ships could destroy the coastal batteries and forts, brush aside any Ottoman naval response in the Sea of Marmara, and appear off the coast of Constantinople, the *Sublime Porte* (the Ottoman Government) would crumble and sue for peace.

Born of the fertile and impatient mind of Winston Churchill, the First Lord of the Admiralty, the idea was based upon an ancient premise that ships could physically brush aside the beetling brows of the Dardanelles coasts without recourse to military action. (Nevertheless, Lord Kitchener, the Secretary of State for War, kept the last regular infantry division, the 29th, in Britain – just in case – portending future action.)

On 19 February, the battleships HMS *Cornwallis* and HMS *Vengeance* opened fire on the stone fortresses at the mouth of the Dardanelles Straits, with mixed success. Another attempt was tried, farther into the Dardanelles, six days later. In fact, Churchill had already alerted the Ottomans to the intentions of the Entente Powers, when he had ordered British – and French – cruisers to test the Ottoman outer defences by naval artillery fire. With the fort at the tip of the peninsula, Seddul Bahr, being severely damaged by an exploding magazine and the Ottomans suffering 150 casualties, the Allies were buoyed with success.

The Ottomans noted the intention of their enemies, and redoubled their efforts to secure the Straits – ultimately laying more mines that would claim Allied ships and jeopardise the whole operation. A month later, on 18 March 1915, the naval campaign was over. Three ships (the *Irresistible*, *Bouvet* and *Ocean*) and many lives were lost. The Allied navies retreated, and the Ottomans set to work defending their coastlines. The need for military landings to neutralise the threats to the naval attack was all too apparent.

The die that would ultimately see the Talley brothers heading to the shores of Gallipoli was cast.

28 February 1915

My darling Parents
  Today has been fine with heavy fall of snow in the morning
and perishing cold strong winds which have cleared up a lot of
the mud. I hear at the end of March sports are being arranged
amongst us, I expect I may try my luck. I also hear we have to
do some more of those early turn outs (mounted) to patrol some
miles I must tell you all particularly later. I was pleased to
see that the papers had news today what with our fleet up the
Dardanelles and the Russians advancing again[54] things ought to
go well with us. I do hope you are all keeping well.
  Ever your loving son

  Percy

3 March 1915

My darling Parents
  Today has been so wet we have only exercised the horses.
The latest rumour is that we move off in two weeks time; where,
nobody knows. They have had this officially at the orderly room.
  Ever your loving son

  Per

---

54 In Galicia, against the Austro–Hungarians, things had been exceedingly difficult for the
    Russians facing the Central Powers.

7 March 1915

My darling Parents

I have just come off main guard. I received your letter and
on it you said write soon well I seem to have written so often
I know for a fact every two days. The latest here is that we
move on the 15th, where to nobody seems to know. It was said to
Gallipoli in Asia Minor, about 130 miles from Constantinople,
but we certainly seem to be moving as we are getting all
things ready for a move at any moment, as for leave am afraid
that is out of the question.

I should have liked to have seen you all before going and
might have been able to obtain a weekend before all this news.
I don't think I should talk about our moving until you hear
from us again, perhaps Mrs Owen has heard something from her
son, I have been speaking to some Middlesex[55] men and they have
been told by their Major that they leave on the 15th. Well
I will say good bye now as I want to have a wash before turning
in early as tomorrow is to be a heavy day.

Ever your loving son

Percy

---

55   1st County of London Yeomanry (Middlesex Hussars), brigaded with the Rough Riders.

8 March 1915

My dear Father

I had intended to have written some time yesterday, but left it late in the hopes of getting some definite news as regards our movements. It is quite certain that we move from here, though whether on the 15th or not nobody knows; but I know that pith helmets, six new tunics and breeches made of Khaki Drill[56] have been ordered for us, so that is sufficient proof that we go to some hot country, as I mentioned before Gallipoli has been suggested, but I suppose Egypt is just as likely.

Today about 20 fresh horses have been brought in, hope I shall get one of them, my own beast is certainly better, I took her out this afternoon for the first time for a week, she was much easier, but any time and as likely to go lame again.

It has been rumoured that we may go to Salisbury Plain for a week or two for a final training, but do not know if it is at all likely; for one thing I should like it, as then we might be able to get home for 48 hours or so as it is we are not likely to get any leave at all, anyhow I will let you know immediately anything definite is given to us.

Ever your affectionate son

Frank

---

56 Wolseley pattern sun helmets were worn by all British troops in hot countries, and were intended to be cool and to provide sufficient shade; Khaki Drill, a cotton uniform that replaced the wool serge, was an 'order of dress' issued for wear in hot countries, and was similar to that worn by the Rough Riders in the Anglo-Boer War.

10 March 1915

My darling Parents

Just a note to tell you we have been told nothing official but everything points this way, the horses are only to be exercised at a walk now no drills or schemes, so you see these things would not be done unless something was on, we have also had new horses, and getting things we are short of. I see May is down here[57] I saw her in the distance when on my horse, will write you as soon as anything definite is settled. I should like to come home see you but am afraid it is out of the question.

Ever your loving son

Percy

17 March 1915

My darling Parents

There is no news here. The latest is that we may have to wait a week or so as the convoys[58] must be allowed to return for us, they have taken thousands of infantry out and cannot spare more convoys hence the delay. The weather here is still very fine, today looked a little threatening but seems to have blown over. The doctor examined our teeth[59] said I had one was a little rocky and I know it as it has been hurting a little. I am sorry I cannot tell you any more news as soon as any comes along will let you know at once.

Ever your loving son

Percy

---

57 May was Frank's new wife.

58 Troop transports to take the Rough Riders overseas.

59 It was essential that soldiers had good teeth; army food could be extremely trying, with the traditional biscuits very hard. Many men were rejected or discharged due to their teeth.

19 March 1915

My dear Mother

Yesterday morning it was raining hard and at 9 o'clock turned
to snow and kept on without stopping until after 5 o'clock. Today
it is thawing hard, so you can imagine the state of the roads,
nothing but pools of water all round and it is too rather cold.

Tonight I am going on picket on the cliff by the White House
so am looking forward to a pretty cold job. I should take my
sleeping hat and put on under my hat, so shall be quite comfortable. My poor old beast is still lame, on Wednesday we went
out on one of our schemes and about 2 miles along the North
Walsham Road she went off so I had to get off and walk home.

It is past time for parade so I must stop, as I shall not have
time to write more after. My new riding breeches are a very
good fit and could not have been made better.

Your affectionate Son

Frank

19 March 1915

Just a card to say I am quite fit. The last two days have been very miserable, snow quite heavy and terrible winds. Tomorrow we have a big day on. Leave I think will be along soon, nothing difficult as regards leaving.
  Love to all

Percy

23 March 1915

No news. I was vaccinated Saturday, no effect so far, I am cook for this week thankful when it is over as I have a headache practically all the week being in the fire.
Love

Per

23 March 1915

My dear Father

There is very little news to give you, today we have been out on a Brigade Scheme, I had to ride my old beast again, which went lame and I had to walk it back between 2 or 3 miles as it took an hour to do it.

There is no more definite news about going yet, but I hear that rubber shoes have been drawn for us to wear on deck.[60] April 12th has been suggested as the date.

Tonight I believe we are to have an alarm, if so we shall have to turn in as we are. I shall be able to find out later, when I go down to the orderly room for orders. I am glad to see in today's paper that the Russians have taken Przemysl[61] back, 30,000 prisoners, it will release a large number of men to add to their other armies. I think soon we shall be having better news and a general collapse of the Kultured[62] Hun.

Ever your affectionate Son

Frank

---

60 On board the troop ships, this would have been unnecessary for a short sea crossing.

61 Przemysl was a major fortress on the Austro-Hungarian–Russian border in Galicia. With the Austro-Hungarian forces falling back, the Przemysl was placed under siege by the Russians. From 24 September 1914 the Austro-Hungarians held out, finally surrendering on 22 March 1915, with the loss of thousands of prisoners.

62 Much was made, in the press, of German '*Kultur*', which, it was said, was wreaking havoc across Europe – and was used as a propaganda tool by the British.

Typhoid was a significant threat to health in 1914–15. Also known as 'enteric fever', the disease was spread by ingesting food or water that had been contaminated by faeces – mostly by the action of flies and other vermin. With such things unavoidable, it was necessary to use inoculations to combat the disease. The method was not without side effects, however, and many men suffered from the injections they were given prior to going overseas. Its effects were described by the distinguished physician Sir William Ostler, in 1916:

> The method has proved of inestimable value … The material used is a bouillon or agar culture of bacilli heated to a temperature of 53° to 55°C. in order to kill them. Three inoculations are given at intervals of ten days. Untoward results are rare. The inoculation fever begins in from four to six hours and may reach 101° or even 103˙10°. Headache, chilliness, pains in the back and limbs, and vomiting may occur. More severe symptoms may occur … A light diet, avoidance of stimulants and rest lessen the possibility of serious sequels. The evidence so far points to a persistence of the protective effect for at least two years after inoculation.[vii]

With Egypt being the probable destination of the 2nd Mounted Division, there were many preparations – inoculations being high up on this list:

> Early in March … the Division was warned for overseas. It was soon known the destination was Egypt, and preparations for the move began. Horses were exercised at a walk only. Deficiencies in kit were made good. A final round of leave was granted. Vacancies in personnel were filled from the Base as fast as they occurred, the Base itself being kept up to strength by drafts from Putney … Finally, all ranks were re-vaccinated, so that many men had their arms in a sling when they embarked.[viii]

24 March 1915

My darling Parents

The last few days I have not been feeling up to the scratch.
It is the vaccination. I am off my food, tired and weak in the
legs but suppose it will soon pass off I was done last Saturday,
Frank today. As regards going, it may be at any moment we heard
all leave was stopped but think this only applied to the leave
which our squadron leader was authorised to give but think it
will come through regimental orders that we shall have our
48 hours. I shall be thankful when this week is over as I am
fed up with this cooking business. This evening has turned
out quite wet, today early, was very warm and misty, I was
simply perspiring while cooking. I hope you are all well at
home. I was pleased to see the good work the Russians had done,
I hope it means they will get a move on to end the war. I will
write you as soon as I hear anything.

Ever your loving son

Percy

26 March 1915

Just a line to tell you I am quite well, I hear we go April 4th,
am trying to do something about leave I shall be disappointed
if I cannot come.

Love

Per

29 March 1915

My dear Mother

I am sorry I have not written for some time I had intended to yesterday but felt very rotten after the vaccination. I was alright until midday on Saturday when I began to feel very cold and shivery and a bad head, just like flu, unfortunately I had to go on guard the same night on the cliff by the White House and that did not improve me, yesterday I was able to take things easily and today I felt much better, my arm is not so very bad but sufficient just to know that it is not quite right.

I don't know whether Percy has told you, that it is definite that we leave here early next. Our Commanding officer General Peyton goes on Saturday as regards leave nothing has been decided yet, and looks as if we may not get any.

I see in your last letter to Percy that you have got us a wristed-watch, many thanks for it.[63] I think perhaps it would be better if you sent them through by post, I have asked Mrs Harvey if she would mind your addressing the parcel to her at Eden Hall so that it will not have to go through our post and she is quite willing, it will also save time, don't post anything in the way of a letter inside, as probably they will open it not knowing your writing, you might put a piece of white paper round the box first to put your name on and address on. Now I must stop as I have to go down the road for orders.

Ever your affectionate son

Frank

---

63 Wristwatches became popular during the war, as it became apparent that they were more convenient to use than the average pocket watch. Before the war, such watches had mostly been the preserve of women. As the war went on wristwatches became 'trench watches', and covers and guards were made to protect the watch crystal on active service.

29 March 1915

My darling Parents

Thank you for your letter it is very good of you to have
bought us both a watch it will be so nice to have the reliable
time. I am feeling almost fit again except for a little irrita-
tion, Frank who was done last Wednesday has not been at all
well, but you need not worry about him. I feel rather uneasy
as regards leave myself I do not think we shall have any, our
General leaves on Saturday, the only leave at present is
special, and only four from each troop allowed to go at a time
for a weekend. I am trying to find out about it all I can so
will let you know as soon as I hear anything, of course don't
attempt to come down again to us as it might spoil our chance.
We are not doing much in the drill line as the vaccinated arms
stops it. In fact one or two have been very ill.

Ever your loving son

Percy

5 April 1915

Arrived safely good journey though rather crowded up to
Ipswich. Letters Percy will have already told you about, watch
also safe and now on my wrist it is a beautie, many thanks
for it. So far fine and warm though windy no further news yet.

Yours

Frank

8 April 1915

My dear Mother

News is scarce with us, otherwise I would have written before. As regards future movements we are still in the dark, though we expect to move anytime after Saturday, though our destination is not known and probably if we are told it will not be until we are on the boat.

Since returning we have had our new saddles, which I think when they get a little softer and pliable will be a great improvement on the old ones. Did you happen to see yesterday's Daily News? On the back page there is a photograph of four of our fellows from B Squadron they are on guard on the cliff by the wreck at Walcott Gap, for once the papers have reproduced a photograph and not the result of a correspondent's imagination. The fellow standing on the right of the picture is named Withers.

The watch as far as I can judge is keeping very good time and is very easy to read at night time, I have managed to get one of the new covers for it, they are made of brass and cover the glass face, so it will I hope keep it from getting damaged. I must go for orders now.

Ever your affectionate son

Frank

8 April 1915

Trooper P.L. Talley
2366
4 Troop
D Squadron
City of Ldn Yeo (Rough Riders)
4th Mounted Brigade
2nd Mounted Division
British Mediterranean Expeditionary Force

My darling Parents,

Just a line to tell you our new address, as you will see it
is a fairly long one. It seems certain that we go off Saturday,
if not I will let you know at once. I have rather a bad throat,
so sore through coughing so much, but think it will soon be
better. I hope you received my card telling of my safe arrival,
I sent off as soon as possible. How is your foot? I do hope you
will nurse it, that it may soon be well.

The watch goes fine, it was most useful to me last night on
guard, as the night was very windy. I expect this will be the
last letter I shall write you from Bacton, I shall let you hear
from me as often as possible so you must not worry if you do not
hear for a time as no doubt letters will take time to arrive
at a destination, and as you know no news is good news you must
remember; if I do go under, well, you must think of me as doing
so like an Englishman should, so cheerful. I will say goodbye
now, with oceans of love to you all.

Ever your loving son

Percy

Percy Talley was right. On the evening of 10 April 'after a rousing and riotous send-off, squadrons marched independently to Mundesley and entrained'.[ix] Egypt was in their sights, and ultimately, Gallipoli.

Notes

i.   Winston Churchill, *The World Crisis 1911–1918*, 1931, p.231.

ii.   William Le Queux, *The Invasion of 1910*, 1906, p.32.

iii.   A.S. Hamilton, *The City of London Yeomanry (Rough Riders)*, 1936, p.24.

iv.   Winston Churchill, *The World Crisis 1911–1918*, 1931, p.259.

v.   *Manual of Military Law 1914*, HMSO, p.388.

vi.   A.S. Hamilton, *The City of London Yeomanry (Rough Riders)*, 1936, p.27.

vii.   Sir W. Ostler, *The Principles and Practice of Medicine*, Butterworth, 1916.

viii.   A.S. Hamilton, *The City of London Yeomanry (Rough Riders)*, 1936, p.28.

ix.   A.S. Hamilton, *The City of London Yeomanry (Rough Riders)*, 1936, p.29.

3

Egypt

The regiment had moved from Norfolk to Avonmouth, part of the Port of Bristol. These docks on the River Severn were an obvious destination as, situated to the far west, they had long supplied the trade with the Atlantic and on to the Mediterranean. From the Port of Bristol, the Rough Riders would make the journey into the Mediterranean and steam to the north coast of Africa, their destination the Egyptian city of Alexandria.

Egypt was significant to the British, for the Suez Canal – that vital lifeline that crosses the Isthmus of Suez – effectively links the North Atlantic to the Indian Ocean:

> The Canal was, indeed, in the popular German phrase, the 'jugular vein' of the British Empire. Half-way between England and India, on the route which was later to be taken by troops from that country and later from Australia and New Zealand, on that followed by the bulk of the trade between Europe on the one side and Asia and Australasia on the other, it was the most vital focal point upon the communications of the world.[i]

Control of the canal was vital to Britain if it was to ensure trade with its vast Indian territory, yet Egypt was nominally a component part of the Ottoman Empire. With tensions in the region, Britain had occupied Egypt since 1882.

Having defeated the Egyptian Army at the Battle of Tel-el-Kebir, the British set about restoring stability to an otherwise politically volatile zone, in order to protect its own interests, and in particular, the security of the canal. With several nations jockeying for position and power over the waterway, in 1888 the Canal Zone was made neutral under the Treaty of Constantinople, though with Britain ensuring its neutrality, by force if needs be.

With the Ottoman Empire siding with the Central Powers in 1914, the British declared a formal protectorate over the whole country, and deposed the leader, the Khedive, replacing him with a man they referred to as the 'Sultan of Egypt'. Now that the Ottomans were formally an enemy, it was of the greatest importance to the British – and the other Entente Powers – to maintain control of both the canal and the country as a whole. For this reason, a strong British force, under Lieutenant General Sir John Maxwell, was stationed in Egypt.

Maxwell had been in Egypt since he had seen action on the Western Front in 1914, but had previously already served some years in the country. For four years from 1908 to 1912 he had commanded the British forces there. In charge of what was termed the Egyptian Expeditionary Force in August 1914, Maxwell would have to fend off requests for reinforcement by other generals in the region – while defending the ultimate target for Ottoman ambitions, the canal itself. He had some 30,000 troops at his disposal, although this number would fluctuate with the arrival of troops destined for other theatres.

That the threat to the canal was a real one was identified by the fact that it had already been under attack. In November 1914, an Ottoman Army Corps was raised in Syria that was to advance on the east bank of the canal, and in early 1915 the attempt was made. Crossing the desert in seven marches – mostly at night – the Ottoman army of 16,000 men reached the canal bank. The German general sent as military advisor to the Turks, Liman von Sanders, was strongly against the plan:

> On the night of February 2–3 [1915] the attacking troops in proper formation and equipped with boats were successfully moved forward as far as the eastern bank of the canal. When the small British post there opened fire, a panic seized upon the Arabian soldiers. Part of the men already embarked jumped from the boats, others dropped the boats and rafts they were carrying. British re-inforcements quickly arrived after fire had been opened. About two Turkish companies had reached the west bank of the canal; some were killed and some captured. In half an hour the Egyptian bank of the canal was so strongly occupied, that further attempts at crossing had to be given up.[ii]

This demonstration left the British, and Maxwell, nervous of further attempts to take the canal – and nuisance raids continued to test the British defences throughout 1915. If that wasn't enough, an Ottoman-fuelled uprising by the Senussi tribe also underlined the need to have sufficient troops in theatre to combat new and continuing threats. And there would be plenty of troops 'passing through' – on their way to Gallipoli, and ultimately, on their way back.

In early 1915, the obvious destination for a cavalry division – and one trained to fight as mounted infantrymen at that – was Egypt. With the possibility of a mobile, mounted division deploying over the vast tract of open country against the Ottomans, the decision was made to despatch the 2nd Mounted Division to help bolster the number of troops available to Sir John Maxwell. But the logistics of sending mounted troops by sea were complex, with men, horses and materiel. The Talleys were heading for sunnier climes.

April 1915

My darling Parents,

I thought I must write you just once more before leaving, which we do on Saturday[64] about 9 in the evening. I have not been feeling at all well, my throat which has been so sore is better, but I have a very bad cold I think flu, which makes me feel rather miserable, but think by the moving it will have nearly gone. Thank you so much for sending the camphor in the useful little bags I have put them into use at once. We had a group photograph taken round at the stables I have told the man to send to you one big and two post cards which I hope will turn out good.

Love to you my dear Parents.

Percy

---

64   Saturday, 10 April 1915.

13 April 1915

Avonmouth

We are now on board just moving off a little way out, think
we move about 2pm. Had a pleasant journey down, eight in a
carriage. This is a picture of our boat[65] rather a nice one, but
if a little cleaner, would be better. I am in a bunk with three
others all in the same section my cold is better although not
gone. We have had gym shoes and slacks served out and I found
great relief in getting in to them. There are about well over
2000 of us on board. The horses have gone on another boat, mine
stood the railway journey quite well, so am in the hope he will
do the sea voyage.

   Love to all

Percy

Don't worry

---

65   The illustration of SS *Scotian* in the picture section is the front face of Percy's card.

The Talley Brothers were fortunate: their trip to Egypt would be aboard a 10,322-ton cruise ship operated by the Allan Line, SS *Scotian*. Originally launched for the transatlantic run by the Holland America Line in 1898, she was bought by the Allan Line in 1911, and had operated the transatlantic route. Designed for passengers, unlike some troop ships, the men were accommodated in cabins, still strictly separated by rank. While the horses, farriers, drivers and grooms – together with their officers – were packed on board the ex-Wilson Line steamer SS *Toronto*, life on board the *Scotian* was hardly that of the average soldier on an average troop ship:

> The routine on board was not exacting. Mornings had to be passed on deck, and were spent in physical exercises, lectures, musketry parades and games. Except for occasional boat- and fire-drills, the rest of the day was free for card-playing, sing-songs and concerts. The ship possessed a canteen of sorts, but its stock was very limited, its service snail-like, and it was all but 'dry'.[iii]

13 April 1915

S.S. Scotian
Allan Line
Avonmouth

My dear Father

After my letter of Saturday I did not expect to write from England again, but you will see we have not made a move up to the present, I believe waiting for some of the other regiments to embark. We have just heard that we may move out of the dock this afternoon and preparations seem to indicate that we may be going although perhaps only to anchor out in the river.

I am in a six bunk cabin, but only five in at present mine is one of the top ones it is only a Second Class boat and we are all forward in the steerage, but fortunately only one floor down, so might be very much worse.

We have had khaki trousers[66] – gym shoes issued and today we have each had a lifebelt given and a place appointed in the lifeboats so perhaps we may get practice at taking up our places on the way out.

Ever your affectionate son

Frank

---

66   The Rough Riders would normally wear breeches and putties. These trousers were
referred to as 'slacks' by the brothers.

14 April 1915

My dear Father

Today the pilot leaves us at 8 o'clock p.m. and will take the letters with him. There is no news of course except that we sail after dark tonight, so that tomorrow morning when we turn out land will be out of sight. It all seems very strange and little did I think that I should leave England under such conditions though I am still convinced that we shall be back home again before Xmas.

Ever your affectionate son

Frank

14 April 1915

My darling Parents

Just a note before we sail we have been on board since Sunday getting ready, and we are all very anxious to be on the move. We rise in the morning 6.30 have breakfast, then physical drill for an hour, at present we are not doing very much. We have had life belts given to us and told off to the different boats, so we all know exactly where to go. I am feeling better, throwing off my cold by degrees. I hear we sail tonight at 8 o'clock all the other transports out here in the bay are getting upstream.

This is a most beautiful spot here in the bay. We were brought here by tugs yesterday evening. I sent you news on two postcards which I hope you will receive, a picture of our boat. We are just off Avonmouth dock, quite near to land which I think is Somerset, perhaps you will be able to find out from the maps? I should like to tell you heaps but I want this to get through to you so am guarded in what I say. Now, my dear Parents, don't worry as this may be the last letter for some time.

Ever your loving son

Per

16 April 1915

My darling Parents,

I thought I would write you a letter so that I may be able to post at our first port of call. When we arrived at Avonmouth on the Sunday we went direct on board after shipping the horses[67] and stayed there until we left Thursday evening. It has been very interesting on board although dull at times, this I mean before starting. When we were brought out to be for a time in the bay it seemed so strange, thinking perhaps it would be the last time we should see the shores of old England, then on the quay the Middlesex and Sharpshooters,[68] gave us a good send off and we shipped each other, of course for the time your thoughts go in other directions.

Well we anchored in the bay for two nights, the night before we left the two torpedo boats which were to escort us came up alongside, of course we went all over them and made friends with the sailors who were indeed fine men and had been in nearly every sea fight. The boats are only 12 months old and can do about 40 miles an hour and the guns have a range of 8000yds, wonderful for such a boat; they say they are simply doing all they can for a fight but the Germans are frightened of these boats. The bay we anchored in was a most beautiful place. I think it was at the mouth of the Severn; there is a school on the front and you could hear quite plainly the cheers they gave as we passed by. Of course we returned them, which did make me think of home, all these cheers coming from such young throats.

Last night Friday everybody had to be below deck and all lights out by 8 o'clock, as we had to go through the danger zone[69] and the torpedo boats had left us only coming about

---

67 On board SS *Toronto*. The *Toronto* would be the first to arrive in Alexandria – leaving much to be done by the Rough Riders on board.

68 Both battalions of the County of London Yeomanry had been accommodated within the docks themselves, and were on hand to see off the first of their brigade to move overseas.

69 The Germans had declared a maritime 'danger zone' around the coast of Britain.

150 miles which is also a very critical part of the journey, of course we do not know where we are going or our first port. We rise at 6.30 have roll call, then we are free till breakfast. Next is a parade about 9 for physical drill which lasts 1 hour, then we are free to do what we like; all sorts of games are played on deck boxing, wrestling, etc., some lie about and read or write.

Lunch starts at about 12 o'clock, in the afternoon there is a rifle inspection, of course there are fatigues and guards, but we are not over worked. I have not been sick yet although have been feeling rather giddy faint and weary and had to go to the doctor, but shall soon get over it no doubt. We are four in our cabin, all nice fellows and in the same section so we get on well together. On board besides the Rough Riders are the A.V.C., A.S.C., R.E.s.[70] Brigadier, Colonel, and all the heads; our boat, which is the Scotian, is quite on its own, but she is a fairly fast boat and can I believe show a good pair of heels if needs be.[71] We were all given a box of 50 cigarettes, don't quite know who was responsible for it but it was quite acceptable.

I am writing you two or three letters, which is really one so do hope you will receive them all. Of course I cannot tell you all that has happened as I want you to have these letters and to know that I am doing alright. Frank at present is as fit as a fiddle, although he had a touch of diarrhoea as dozens of the fellows did - self included. All night-long you could hear people running about so in the morning there was a big parade before the doctor who gave them a dose of castor oil to clear germs out of the stomach, which I think did them all a deal of good. Please excuse the scribble and punctuation as I feel rather giddy and must stop writing for the time being.

---

70 Army Veterinary Corps, Army Service Corps and Royal Engineers – all essential components of the 2nd Mounted Division.
71 The threat from submarines was ever present.

Today is Sunday and a glorious one, sun shining brightly and so hot everybody is lying about the deck. This morning we had church parade and I think there is another this evening. Expect we shall arrive at Gibraltar tomorrow morning. So far about seven other ships have passed us; it did seem so strange at first to look over the water and see no signs of life, but you soon get use to it. I have actually had a smoke today the first for two days, so you see I am getting my sea legs there has been hardly any sickness on board of course we have been very fortunate, as we have had no heavy seas so far. Hope you have received the photo we had taken at Bacton before leaving.

Ever your loving son

Percy

18 April 1915

My dear Mother

I have not written a portion of my letter every day, as news is not plentiful and as I believe they are to be censored we cannot say too much.

We have been fairly fortunate regarding weather having only had one wet night. Today has turned out glorious and hot, this is due, I suppose to our nearing the Mediterranean. We are due to pass Gibraltar sometime tomorrow and hope it will be during the day, as should like to catch a glimpse of the place, and also hope we may be able to get our letters ashore.

The journey has been very successful on the whole. I felt a little queer on Friday but have quite got over that and feel OK now. Percy was also bad and I think rather rotten but he too is now much better, fortunately it has been calm otherwise we should have been very much worse.

This morning we had a church parade not very long which
I was rather glad of, as the sun was boiling hot and we were
all jammed up together in the stern and we now all make a rush
for the coolest spots. We are not getting very much work to do,
it is almost impossible with the number of men on board, what
I like best is the hours physical exercise we get in the morning it has made me feel very fit and I quite look forward to it.

Washing accommodation is not great for so many, but if it were
possible to get even a cold bath it would not be so bad, I shall
endeavour to get one, if it is to be had. Please excuse the paper
being dirty, but I have had to chase some of it round the deck,
it would be very much easier to write down stairs, but it is so
awfully stuffy there that we never go down when it is for meals.

You will find Percy's letter has been opened he has just
heard that they are to be handed in open so have to come to me
for an envelope, what on earth they want to read the letters
for at this period I don't know, as we cannot possibly give any
military information away, especially as we don't even know
where we are going to.

Love to all, yours

Frank

Leaving Avonmouth on 15 April, the *Scotian* picked its way carefully around the Iberian Peninsula on its journey to the Aegean. The danger from German submarines was all too apparent. Originally escorted by two destroyers, the liner was left to its own devices, so for the men aboard – aware of the loss of other ships – it was a nervy experience. Just four days before, SS *Wayfarer*, with 200 men and horses of the 1st Warwickshire Yeomanry – also bound for Egypt as part of the 2nd Mounted Division – had been attacked 60 miles west of the Scilly Islands. Torpedoed by the U-32, the *Wayfarer* was damaged, though fortunately casualties were light, with two men and five horses killed. The ship was towed to Queenstown and was later repaired in Liverpool.

The surviving Warwicks would arrive in Egypt and would ultimately take their position in the line at Suvla Bay. The near loss of the *Wayfarer* spawned a number of rumours about the passage of the *Scotian*.

The danger presented by the Atlantic passed as the ship sighted first the town of Tarifa, at the tip of Spain, in the Strait of Gibraltar, with the comforting sight of 'The Rock' in the distance:

> Tarifa was sighted about noon on the 19th. Shortly afterwards Gibraltar was passed, but at such a distance that the squat rock seen dimly through the haze hardly seemed a 'Pillar of Hercules.' The glory of the first Mediterranean sunset, however, and the phosphorescence on the sea brought everyone on the deck.[iv]

Not stopping, the *Scotian's* intermediate destination was the magnificent natural Grand Harbour of Valetta, in Malta. This island, in the centre of the Mediterranean, was an important staging post for the British – especially with their activities in Egypt, Gallipoli and subsequently, Salonika. Malta was also significant as 'the nurse of the Mediterranean', with, by the end of the war, some twenty-seven military hospitals established that would cater for the wounded of Gallipoli, Salonika and other campaigns.

Tempting as they looked from the decks of the *Scotian*, the evident delights of Malta were strictly off limits, for most soldiers, at least:

> Reaching Malta on the 22nd, the Scotian put into the Grand Harbour, Valetta, to fill up with coal and water. Only the officers were allowed to land, but the men spent the day exploring through field glasses, bartering with the bumboat-men, and watching the gondola-like dghaisas darting in and out among the shipping.[v]

22 April 1915

Malta Harbour
On board S.S. Scotian

We entered the harbour this morning about 11.30, awfully
interesting but fails description, have hoped to get ashore for
a couple of hours, but no luck so far. Have been surrounded by
boats, about 100 in all.[72] Are about to start coaling?
  Love to all, yours

  Frank

22 April 1915

My darling Parents
  We have just arrived at Malta, and am just sending this card
in case you do not receive my letters and cards. Physical drill
has been called, so that we may see everything, at the present
we are both very fit and well.
  Oceans of love

  Percy

We have had an ideal voyage

---

72 Maltese boatmen, aware of their captive customers, plied a trade in the Grand Harbour
    at Valetta, supplying soldiers with postcards, fruit and all manner of goods.

Leaving Malta behind, the *Scotian* steamed on to the Greek island of Lemnos, just 30 miles off the coast of Gallipoli. Arriving at the natural harbour of Mudros on 25 April, the Rough Riders were only too aware that they might be directly embroiled in the landings on this hostile coast. Rumours were rife, particularly when the ship left the harbour three days later, bound for the peninsula itself. The men on board busied themselves with drills and letter writing.

28 April 1915

My dear Mother

We have suddenly been warned that a mail is to leave shortly and there has been a stampede to our cabin for writing paper and envelopes, as we have been anchored since Sunday in a most glorious bay and thought that we should have the chance of getting any letters away.

We are having glorious weather and the sea this morning is like glass, but we are getting rather tired of our confinement quarters and shall be glad to get on land again. Owing to the censorship it is impossible to give details that we should like to and therefore makes letter writing rather difficult. Time is now up so I must stop.

Love to all yours

Frank

Both very fit and well

28 April 1915

My darling Parents

It is now 8 o'clock and here there is a mail at 9, so am just scribbling you a note to tell you we are both quite fit and well. We hear quite a lot of rumours here and one is that our ship has gone down, well it has not – we heard that this had got into the London papers.[73]

We are still on board hidden in a little bay[74] and as to our movements nobody knows anything. Am afraid our letters will not be newsy as we dare not say more than we are quite safe, as the letters may be destroyed. Don't listen to any rumours about ships being sunk and as far as I can see letters may be few and far between; don't worry, specially at the present, as we are rather cut off from things. Remember our address and you have a good idea as to our position; at times we hear the guns.

Ever your loving son

Percy

From Lemnos, the *Scotian* and its human cargo moved offshore from the Gallipoli Peninsula, arriving to see the struggles of the 29th Division pressing forward up the slopes at Cape Helles towards the village of Krithia and the heights of Achi Baba, thought to dominate the Narrows of the Dardanelles. Rumours were rife that the Rough Riders would put ashore; if that was to be the case, they would be landed as infantry – the *Toronto* had already arrived at Alexandria and was offloading its cargo of horses and equipment. In any case, the Talley brothers were in time to observe battle in progress – before finally moving on to Egypt.

---

73 Presumably nervousness following the attack on the *Wayfarer*.
74 Mudros, a natural but then under-used harbour at Lemnos.

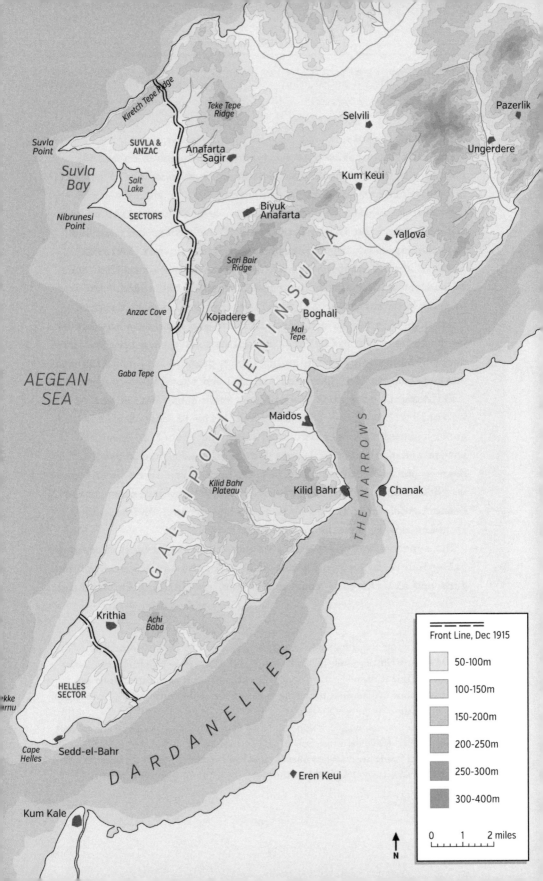

Kiretch Tepe Ridge

Teke Tepe Ridge

Selvili

Pazerlik

Suvla Point

SUVLA & ANZAC

Ungerdere

Anafarta Sagir

Suvla Bay

Kum Keui

Salt Lake

SECTORS

Biyuk Anafarta

Nibrunesi Point

Yallova

GALLIPOLI PENINSULA

Sari Bair Ridge

Anzac Cove

Kojadere

Boghali

Mal Tepe

AEGEAN SEA

Gaba Tepe

Maidos

THE NARROWS

Kilid Bahr Plateau

Kilid Bahr

Chanak

DARDANELLES

Krithia

Achi Baba

HELLES SECTOR

kke rnu

Cape Helles

Sedd-el-Bahr

Eren Keui

Kum Kale

Front Line, Dec 1915

50–100m

100–150m

150–200m

200–250m

250–300m

300–400m

0   1   2 miles

N

5 May 1915

My darling Parents

You will be surprised to hear that we have been on board
nearly a month, of course we do not know when we shall get off,
but we arrive at Alexandria tomorrow.

We have had quite an exciting time, we have been right up to
the fighting line in the Dardanelles. Our troops only landed
last Sunday week, the fighting was terrible, you will hardly
believe what I am about to say, but it has been worse than Mons.
We had certain troops on board which had to be landed,[75] so
we have been kept near all the fighting, shells have dropped
quite close to us. We could see our men and horses on the land,
we could hear the rifle fire, aeroplanes have been over us and
dropped bombs, so you see we have seen quite a lot. The firing of
our battleships[76] is wonderful and my word the noise is terrific.

Fighting is done mostly at night, when a big battle was on
we would all go up on board and watch the flashes from the
guns, some of our fellows could hear the cheers on land the
losses are truly terrible, as I have already said worse than in
France. We are not required yet awhile, there is no base formed
we should only be in the way, no doubt we shall come on the
scene later. It would be so nice to see a paper and hear what
is going on, we have been absolutely cut off.

The sunsets are beautiful I cannot describe them such wonderful colours, to be seeing all this and yet hear the roar of the
guns and all the time your countrymen are falling in thousands

---

75 Sappers of the Royal Engineers, and naval personnel. Captain Wedgwood Benn of the
Middlesex Hussars recalled: 'The Roughriders ... had enjoyed a splendid spectacular
view of one of the preliminary bombardments, and when we met them again in
Egypt some of them were beginning to show traces of the "narrow shave" infection in
conversation.' *In the Side Shows*, p. 13.

76 'When an ear-splitting explosion resounded through the ship, everyone tumbled from
his bed and feared the worst, only to find on reaching the deck that it was the "*Queen
Elizabeth*" using her main armament against some remote target!' A.S. Hamilton, *City
of London Yeomanry (Rough Riders)*, 1936, p. 33.

seems almost, well ... A long dreary fight is in front of us here, we shall need many more men if we are to conquer, although everybody is very confident.

I wish I could only describe to you a little more fully but dare not. I will say this that the enemy are very cunning, they had actually got barbed wire in the water which of course stopped our little boats, the courage of our men is wonderful. I believe if they had lost their heads while landing they would have been wiped out; instead they were up and at them and made two bayonet charges in ten minutes, so secured a landing. Some of our fellows have been fortunate to row the officers ashore,[77] so of course had a good look around.

I do hope you have received my cards and letters I have written quite a lot. We are both well although of course not as fit as one might be after such a time on board. Will you please tell anybody the contents of this note who might be interested. I am writing this on a nasty hard wooden table in our mess room, so excuse the scribble. One poor chap (not our regiment) died, we had to bury him at sea.[78] How are you all keeping? Well I hope, and not worrying about us, as of course when we have to leave again for fighting you may not hear from us for a very long time.

Ever your loving son

---

77 'Of what was happening ashore no authentic news reached the ship, but from officers who went sight-seeing, the men who rowed them, and the crews of lighters which came alongside, something was learned of the bitter fighting and the crippling losses.' A.S. Hamilton, *City of London Yeomanry (Rough Riders)*, 1936, p.32.

78 SE/559 Private Ernest William Scutt, 11th Veterinary Section, Army Veterinary Corps, died of pneumonia and was buried at sea on 3 May 1915; he is commemorated on the Chatby Memorial, Alexandria.

In his regimental history, A.S. Hamilton, himself a Rough Rider, adds further dimension to Percy's story of observing the shores of Gallipoli. On 28 April 1915, the *Scotian* was moored off the coast of the peninsula, close to HMS *Queen Elizabeth* and Gully Beach beyond:

> With terrific din every warship was blazing away shorewards with every gun that could be brought to bear. The crest of Achi Baba was hidden in a halo of bursting shell; Krithia smouldered under a huge, black pall; burning scrub sent heavy clouds creeping along the ground, while shrapnel bursts marked the front lines and the main avenues of approach. Apart from the smoke, however, little could be seen; the cliff top hid most of the country nearest the shore, and the beach was so crowded that, although the view was uninterrupted, one could not see the wood for the trees. With nightfall, the bombardment died down, and the First Battle of Krithia came to an end.[vi]

6 May 1915

Are just arriving in view of Alexandria, and am sending this in advance of a letter as we may not get time for a day or two to write, so will keep all news until then. Both very fit but shall be glad to get off the boat.
  Love to all, yours

  Frank

9 May 1915

. City Beach
. Alexandria

My dear Father

We arrived here on Friday, after leaving the boat we had a terrible march through the town of about an hour in full marching order in blazing sun before we reached the team. At present we are only about 300 yards away from the sea and get two dips a day, which is a great blessing.

Our work is done early in the morning, we get up at 5 o'clock and go out for horse exercise, returning at 7.15 and get our own breakfast at 7.30. Then if we are lucky enough to dodge the fatigues, we have nothing further to do until midday stables at 11.45; during this time we have our first dip, the same happens in the afternoon.

At lunch we only have bread and cheese and tea, and one meat for the last meal at 6.30, which is a very good idea, as it is so hot that we do not feel like eating much. Oranges are plentiful and fairly cheap, five for 1 piastre, which is about equal to 2½d. In a week or two we are to move off to a place called Ismailia, somewhere on the Canal.

Yesterday evening I went into the town of Alexandria, chiefly to get a new watch glass, as had unfortunately broken it, but it did not affect the watch at all and still keeps beautiful time.

Love to all, yours

Frank

9 May 1915

My darling Parents,

After going to the Dardanelles, we are now at Alexandria in
Camp. My word it is awful, what with the heat and sand, one
thing we are near the sea and can pop down for a swim, which
I have done everyday and felt the benefit of. I think we move
off in a short time to a place very much hotter, don't believe
any reports you may hear about our transports, we had quite a
safe journey. I wrote you a long letter telling you everything
that happened which I hope you received.

I hope to go into Alexandria this evening we are situated about
9 miles away, it is not much of a place from what I could see as
we marched through, and from what I have heard. Father's letter
came to us here at Sidi Bishr (our camp) on the 7th. I loathe this
camp life. My horse is quite fit and seems in a better condition
than when in England, we lost over thirty horses,[79] one or two
have died here on land. The natives here are a funny lot make
an awful noise, will do you right and left, you have to bargain
with them, and if they don't agree to your price you tell them
to clear off or threaten to hit them. I will try and write you a
long letter later on at present I am fed up.

Ever your loving son

Pex

---

79 'The horses were all on the decks, and for those in the bowels of the ship [the *Toronto*]
the atmosphere was appalling … It was not surprising therefore that the septic
pneumonia the remounts had brought on board soon spread to the Regiment's
horses … two or three horses a day succumbed.' A.S. Hamilton, *City of London
Yeomanry (Rough Riders)*, 1936, p.34.

9 May 1915

Percy Talley
Telegram, Eastern Telegraph Co

TALLEY TELCON LN
OWING TO RUMOURS WIRING BOTH FIT BEEN
DARDANELLES NOW ALEXANDRIA = TALLEY

10 May 1915

My darling Parents
   Just a note to say we are moving again tomorrow, I hope you
received my wire saying we were safe. It is has been very hot
again today, the flies are terrible crawling all over you. Our
clothes and boots are white with sand. I often think of you
specially when I look at my watch, it is most useful. I do not
know what I should do without it.
   Ever your loving son

   Percy

Arriving at Alexandria on 10 May 1915, the Rough Riders were reunited with their horses and the personnel that had been despatched to Egypt with them on board SS *Toronto*. From their location on the shores of the Mediterranean the City yeomen moved quickly to the Suez Canal, travelling the 200 miles to take their place alongside the other defenders of this strategically important waterway. Their first destination was the town of Ismailia, close to Lake Timsah, and then, for B and D squadrons at least, farther south to Port Suez, where the canal meets the Red Sea.

The British defences were arranged along the west bank of the canal, originally in the belief that the inhospitable terrain of the Sinai Peninsula would be too much for any attacker. This had proven not to be the case following the Ottoman assault in February, and the enemy continued to threaten to test the defences. The Rough Riders were needed to bolster the British presence on the canal and on their arrival were added to the reserve of Indian Army troops already on site, becoming the first British troops to be stationed there.

On their arrival on 11 May, the Rough Riders were placed in reserve, in the trying conditions of a fly-blown tented camp. Arthur Hamilton, then a lance corporal in the Rough Riders, described the scene:

> New Camp, where the reserve was stationed, lay behind the town astride the old caravan road to Cairo. Open desert surrounded the camp on three sides and this, though mostly firm and becoming gravelly as one went inland, yet contained much powdery dust, which swirled through the camp in sand-pipes, enveloped men and horses on parades, and permeated everywhere. At first the Regiment was lodged in single-fly bell-tents, so that during the day helmets were as necessary inside as out.[vii]

The Talley brothers soon settled down to the routine of a yeomanry regiment in the desert. Captain Wedgwood Benn, of the 1st County of London Yeomanry, brigaded with the Rough Riders, recorded his experiences of the camp:

> The day's work commenced very early, sometimes at half-past four or five, with a parade. By eight o'clock the sun was up and we were home to breakfast. Thereafter there were 'stables' and two waterings of the horses, but after stables those who were not told off for watering had little to do for the rest of the day. I soon made the discovery that the great heat had the power of sapping all energy.[viii]

15 May 1915

Port Suez

My dear Mother

Thanks for your letter, which reached us at Alexandria.
I think I told you in my letter sent from there, that we
expected to get sent off to Ismailia, instead last Tuesday we
got pushed off to the above town, which is the hottest place
I have yet been to, and ever want to go to either.

Our hours of work are the same as at Alexandria, up at 5 and
work till 8 o'clock and then unless we are on any fatigue we do
nothing until 12 o'clock and then again until 5 o'clock, but we
find it quite enough to do to keep still and keep the flies off.

We are about 20 minutes walk from the town itself and about
200yds from the Canal on a nice sandy plain, so that when we
get anything of a breeze we get plenty of dust thrown in.

I shall not give any news, as all letters are to be censored,
so will only say that we are both fit and well and hope in a
little time to get more accustomed to the heat. All details
will have to remain until our return.

Love to all, yours

Frank

15 May 1915

My darling Parents,

I hope you read my cable from our last destination,[80] we are
some miles from there now. It is very, very, hot and the
flies numerous, between the two life at times, at least to me,
is almost unbearable; you know how I suffer from the heat, at
night it generally blows hard and the sand is enough to suf-
focate you. We have had strict instructions as to giving any
information regarding our position, movements, troops, etc,
so you see I cannot write you a very interesting letter at
present. The only thing is that we are both fit although at
times your stomach gets out of order, but you have to get used
to such trifles.

Ever your loving son

Per

Note added by censor
Your son is near Suez

---

17 May 1915

Hear there is another post, so am just sending this card,
I sent a letter on Sunday which I expect you will receive by
this. This card does not denote where we are. I have had my
hair cut off and doubt if you would recognise me now, the heat
still continues and my dress is a shirt and pair slacks, so you
can guess how hot it is.

Yours

Per

---

80 Alexandria.

22 May 1915

My dear Mother

It is difficult to give much news of one's doings when our
letters are censored, as to where we are my last letter will
have told you if it has reached you, and now I can only say we
are still in the same place, and doing much the same with each
day, and, so far as we can gather, we are likely to be here for
an indefinite period, and therefore not likely to do anything
in the fighting line at all.

If our local Egyptian Mail reports are true, Italy has at
last joined in with us;[81] this is only what we have been waiting
for a long time and now that it has come, only hope it may mean
far more to our side than we expected.

As far as we are concerned we are both very fit, but fed up
with the sun, sand and heat, and we miss the bathing we had
at Alexandria. It is now nearly time for midday stables, so I
must stop.

Love to all, yours ever

Frank

---

81 Italy joined the Entente Powers, formally declaring war on Austria–Hungary
    on 23 May 1915, though it had revoked the Triple Alliance (with this country
    and Germany) on 3 May.

22 May 1915

My darling Parents

I was so pleased to receive all your letters yesterday, they all came together, those dated 29th April and May 6th. While writing this letter the perspiration is simply pouring off me and I only have a shirt on, you must keep your helmet on even when in your tent, the sun is so powerful and of course all our work is done early morning. We rise at 4.30, the rest of the day, unless you are on guard or a fatigue, you may do much as you like, the only thing to do is to keep in your tent, of course you must go down to stables at 12 and 5 which last about one hour at each time. I do wish I could write you more fully but it is of no use as it would be stamped out, and perhaps I might have to write the letter again. Frank is in a tent about 20 yards away, so we see quite a lot of each other. Things are very expensive and money runs away like water, Gold Flake cigarettes cost 1/8 for 50. I must go, I have to fall in for stables.

Ever your loving son

Percy

26 May 1915

The heat today is unbearable, hottest we have had and what little breeze there is, is quite warm, it is like opening an oven door. Inside some of our tents it registers 109 degrees.

Cannot write more

Love to all

Per

29 May 1915

My dear Father

Many thanks for the offer of tobacco, etc. but so far I think we are all right. Personally I am not doing much in the smoking world, I suppose the heat.puts one off it, we are now getting it pretty hot 108 in the shade. This we have heard will last another month, so have a good time to look forward to.

You must have had a pretty lively time in London with the Germans, it is a pity it was not done long ago, all of them right to be locked up.[82] Italy I am glad to see has at last joined in and hope it will help considerably to bring matters to a speedy end; she seems, according to the paper we get here each morning (the Egyptian Mail) to be well prepared as regards her supply of artillery and munitions, this no doubt was the cause of her keeping back for such a long time. Owing to Mr Censor[83] we are rather handicapped for news, and when we have said we are both fit and the weather hot, we exhaust all that we feel we can say in safety, to ensure our letters getting through.

I have been sitting for about ½ hour without writing anything and now there are about seven fellows in the tent kicking up an awful row, so writing is rather difficult especially with a lack of news. There is nothing to report about our doings, we are still in camp at the same place and very much fed up with the existence whether we even do anything more is very uncertain as far as we know.

The light is getting bad now and as I shall not have time to add anything tomorrow before the mail goes I must post now.

Yours ever

Frank

---

82 After the sinking of RMS *Lusitania* in early May 1915, there were widespread anti-German riots across Britain. On 12 May 1915, Prime Minister Herbert Asquith announced a policy of 'segregation and internment' of enemy aliens. By November 1915, some 32,440 men had been interned, and some 10,000 older men, women and children 'repatriated' to their country of origin.

83 Soldiers' letters were censored by their officers.

2 June 1915

Just a card to tell you I am still fit although feeling the heat very
much. You might send a paper now and then a Mirror for preference;
we can only buy the Egyptian Mail, which is not much of a paper.
  Love to all

  Per

5 June 1915

My darling Parents

Your letter of 20th May received yesterday, in it you ask what happened to us at the Dardanelles. Well I wrote you a long letter just before landing at Alexandria telling you everything that happened to us, and what we saw; but presume I said too much, this being the reason you have not received it.[84] Of course we are not at Alexandria now, but about 250 miles away, which I told you in one of my letters. One of our Squadrons has been under fire, a rumour, whether it will be our luck or not I don't know, I wish we could, the life here is very monotonous.

The only thing our squadron is fighting is the flies, and a change from this would be most acceptable. The postcards I send will tell you where we are I have sent you many and trust by this time you have received them. You might send a paper now and then, it does not matter where we are, expect we shall receive them. You might let me know anything about the Stock Exchange, about my people if you can. You ask in your letter the reason we left the Dardanelles, it seems they do not want cavalry yet, while there we saw the bombardment it was terrific and one or two of the enemy's shells dropped quite close to us, they also dropped bombs from aeroplanes but of course no damage was done. Of course I could write you an interesting description but had better not risk it.

Ever your loving son

Per

---

84 Despite Percy's fears over censorship, the letter did arrive.

13 June 1915

Suez

My dear Mother

I have very little time for writing this week, in the ordinary way I want until Friday when we generally get some of our
mails, but this week we went out for a night march so have lost
a day, now the mail bag closes in a few minutes.

Percy has sent an Indian Field Service P.C.[85] this mail; don't
think by this that we are doing anything serious, as we are
not, he also is pressed for time and it is a curio. We are still
in the same place[86] and getting a little more accustomed to the
heat, and as far as possible the flies, the latter are only
troublesome during the heat of the day, especially when we are
trying to rest during the day. At night, however, they disap-
pear altogether, so don't worry us.

Thank Father also for the papers he has sent, we are glad to
have them to read, though we get a little news every day as to
how things are going on, I see in our papers the Egyptian Mail
that a Frenchman is agitating for the Japanese to send troops
to France. I wonder if anything will come of it?[87]

I hope now that our letters will reach far quicker now that the
mail service is to be sent through France. I must stop now and
rush for the bag. We are both still very fit and with love to all.
Yours

Frank

---

85   Field Service Postcards were pro forma cards that required the sender to strike out the
     phrases that did not apply in their case; these cards were used as a convenient means of
     letting the people at home know that their loved one was safe. However, as they were
     often sent prior to, or after, an engagement, they could be associated with a difficult
     time 'at the front'. Percy's card is illustrated in the picture section.
86   New Camp, Port Suez.
87   The Japanese, allies of France and Britain, operated mostly in Asia and the Pacific.

Army Form A2042

Nothing is to be written on this except the date and signature of the sender.

Sentences not required may be erased.

If anything else is added the post card will be destroyed.

I am quite well.

~~I have been admitted into hospital~~

~~Sick~~   ~~and am going on well and I hope to be discharged soon~~

~~Wounded~~

~~I am being sent down to the base.~~

I have received your ~~telegram~~

      letter.

      ~~parcel.~~

Letter follows at first opportunity.

~~I have received no letter from you~~ lately

    ~~for a long time~~

Date *13th June 1915*   Signature *Percy*

G.S. & Sons, Calcutta.

Camp routine was monotonous, under trying conditions, but order was restored and training resumed in May, with parades in the morning and evening, and lectures after breakfast. In the heat of the afternoon there was little to do but sit out of the glare of the sun. Occasional night operations were tried. With horses susceptible to ingesting sand, it was necessary to maintain them in good health at all times. This could be a dangerous pastime, as Percy Talley was to find out.

17 June 1915

My darling Parents

You will see by the address that I am in hospital. I spent a day in the camp hospital, then came on to the one in the town. On Monday at Regimental Drill I got a most awful kick by our troop leader's horse. I fell off into the arms of one of the fellows who came to help me, I got it just below the knee which is very lucky; my leg and knee are much swollen and a most ghastly colour, I cannot walk, I was brought here by motor ambulance and carried up on a stretcher. In the same room is a blue jacket[88] who has been operated on for rupture. In another bed is a civilian, a Frenchman I think who has had his leg amputated below the knee. The blue jacket very kindly showed me his cuts, also I have seen the stump, not pleasant sights, he groans terrible when having it dressed.

The heat is tremendous, yesterday, I lay with a sheet over me and a thin net and yet the perspiration was running off me, our guard heat registered 150 the other day, it is truly terrible. It would be nice if some of you could pop in and have a chat. I should like it so much. The day before this I stopped one in the face when on stable guard but I only got a thick nose and cut lip, so taking things all round have been very lucky. I had to come to hospital because a kick like I have wants very careful attention in case water on the knee sets in.[89] You must not worry about me as no doubt by the time you receive this I hope to be about again. I do not feel like writing more, as it is such an effort in bed.

Ever your loving son

Per

---

88 A sailor.

89 'Water on the knee' is the body's reaction to an injury to the ligaments, in order to surround the injured area with protective liquid.

20 June 1915

My dear Father

I cannot thank you for the letters received this week, as the small mail that came in did not contain any from you, only the papers dated June 1–2nd. Perhaps they will come along in a day or so.

I suppose you, like others, heard the effect of the Zeppelin raid at Muswell Hill;[90] fortunately they did not come any nearer, you remember the fellow, Martin, Percy introduced to you at Bacton, he heard in a letter from home, that houses in the next street to his were seriously damaged.

I am sorry to say Percy has had rather a nasty kick from a horse, fortunately it is not serious, though it has forced him to keep to his bed for some time, so to make him comfortable they sent him to the hospital near by where he can have a bed and decent grub. I went down to see him yesterday afternoon and he was much better and seemed quite happy and cheerful, there is absolutely no need for you to worry about him, and by the time you have got this letter he will have been back again to us.

We are getting a little more accustomed to the heat, though at times it is trying, specially when the temperature is about 150 in our tents, which was the case last time I looked. I wish I could give you fuller details of our work and surroundings but it is not much good doing that as I should have to write the letter again, on the other hand we are not doing anything very startling, and seem to be a fixture here.

You will remember Ray Lumb. May tells me he has got a commission in a South Lancashire regiment, whether he is only commencing his training or going straight out to France I have not heard. Grub has just been shouted us so will go.

Yours ever

Frank

---

90 The first Zeppelin raid over London was that of LZ–28, which attacked the city on 31 May 1915. Flying over the northern suburbs, the airship dropped some ninety incendiary devices, and thirty grenades. In all the raid killed seven civilians and injured thirty-five more.

21 June 1915

In Hospital at Suez

My darling Parents,

  I have just posted to Alice.[91] Since doing so I have had my leg
cut the stuff that came out was awful like jelly, but it is so much
easier, I am glad it has been done. I asked the doctor how much
longer he thought I should be before coming out, he said about 10
days or 2 weeks, if that is so, I shall have done nearly 3 weeks in
hospital all through a beastly kick. The cut is about 1 inch long
and ½ inch deep, it looks very healthy, and the colours of my leg
are grand, quite a sight. An Australian lighthouse man shaved my
leg, he is here in hospital having been down with pneumonia.

  June 22. Your letter of June 4th received but no parcel as yet
perhaps Frank has it and will bring on to me. The food things
will be most acceptable; a few cigarettes would have been nice,
although the Egyptian we buy are cheaper than London ones they
are not so nice. Gold Flake costs 1/8 for 50, which is awful.

  The mark on the letter was made, from your description of
the name, by our Captain E. Percy.[92] For washing we do quite
well, paying so much a week, and will write when I want any
new clothes. You must not worry about the raids.[93] I know it is
terrible, but keep calm if any should come your way, I will
certainly think of you all and that no harm will come to you.
The parcel has come and Frank has brought my share round to
the hospital, it is very sweet of you. Think we receive all
your letters, my remark about the telegram perhaps I made
too soon. Don't forget to mention about my money. Don't think
things are going well with us in the Dardanelles,[94] they seem

---

91 The Talley brothers' younger sister.

92 Officers were required to censor the letters of their soldiers, and to indicate this had
    taken place, would sign the envelope.

93 Referring to the Zeppelin raids over London; total casualties inflicted by airships over
    Britain during the war was some 1,914, of which 556 were killed.

94 Percy's comment is accurate; the campaign was heading towards stalemate at
    Cape Helles by this stage of the war.

to be fighting over the same hills as when we were there.

Ever your loving son

Per

---

26 June 1915

Hospital Suez

My darling Parents

I am still in bed making my 12th day there, my leg seems to be getting on well and think the doctor is pleased; am now wait-ing for him to come and see me. I asked the sister if I could get up she said she would ask the doctor, but did not think he would allow me yet. The cake was quite good, the sweets had turned tougher, of course, the paste sarnies will be quite alright. Wallie,[95] in his letter to us, asks if we would like papers sent to us. I forgot to answer; well, we are always most pleased to have papers from anybody. Frank is coming in today to see me. Of course I do not have any news to tell you lying here in bed. Am sending a few photos one of our fellows took which thought might interest you, you will not find me in any of them, although in some I must be quite near, hope they will come safely through as our Major has passed them all. He has about 100 in all, wish I could buy them all, but they cost 3s each. The doctor has just been to see me and is quite pleased, and has let me get up, but I feel very shaky and my knee is a trifle stiff, but shall soon be fit again. I do trust that you are all keeping well at home and whatever you do don't worry about me.

Ever your loving son

Per

---

95   Walter, Percy's older brother.

29 June 1915

Hospital Suez

My darling Parents

Your letters, also papers, parcel all received safely and am
now looking forward to the cigarettes. Don't think me piggy, but
they will be acceptable; Gold Flake, as I say are expensive,
and the Egyptian ones – even the best – are rotten. You ask what
we do of an evening? Well I might say nothing; it gets dark
about 7 o'clock, practically no twilight, the only thing to do
is to go into one of the wooden mess rooms and write, or perhaps
go to the Canteen and turn in early. If you are very flush you
go into town, (you have to get a pass for this) and have a good
blow out, which costs you 2/6 to 5/- which as you see costs too
much, especially on Wednesdays and Saturdays, which are half
holidays. You may leave camp at 2pm returning 10pm, which means
of course tea, and by the time night comes you have spent about
5/-. Result is I don't go in often. As for the so-called town,
there is absolutely nothing to see, of course the first time it
is interesting but after once seen never forgotten. This com-
pletes two weeks with my bad leg, glad to say it is going on
although discharging and will continue to do so, I am afraid,
for some time but no need to worry, there is still plenty of go
in me yet for an olden, my bones must be made of iron.

I have just witnessed an awful sight, this civilian patient
in my ward, suddenly started calling out. I went to find
somebody to come to him, and when I came back the bed was
simply covered in blood, one or two of us stayed by him until
the doctor came, he immediately operated on his legs, meantime
I went to tea, and could see from where I sat, the doctor had
got his hand right in and was cutting away (the leg is cut off
just below the knee as I told you in my last letter) from here
this was opened back to the knee. Of course I need not have
watched this but thought it good for me, a most terrible sight,
he is now coming to. I shall be glad to get out of this, but
perhaps it is all for the best. Some of the sights here are

awful, the wounded I mean, will not go into any more details.
Ever your loving son

Per

3 July 1915

My dear Mother

I don't quite know why your letters do not come in the usual
way with our biggest delivery at the end of the week, but
generally at the beginning as a rule our mail is sent out from
here on a Sunday at least as far as we know, so we have to wait
over a week before we can reply.

The first of the papers with the new wrappers came today,
I have not opened them yet, but shall probably be taking them
down to Percy at the hospital tomorrow. I am glad to say, when
I saw him on Saturday last he was much better and beginning to
hobble about, and no doubt will soon be back again. I should have
gone down to see him again during this week but have had no time.
Wednesdays and Saturdays are the best times for going as they are
our half-day and visiting hours are between 3 and 5 o'clock.

I am sorry to say his horse has kicked the bucket, peritonitis was the cause.[96] It was only ill for 2 or 3 days, whether due
to the sand, which is always flying about I know not, he will
be very upset about it, as he was always asking how it was and
who was riding it in his absence, so I may not tell him tomorrow, unless he is coming back soon.

I think I told you my old beast was left behind at Bacton;
the one I got next was not good for drill, it would not walk,
but was always on the jog and throwing up its head. So unless
I sat well back, it would catch me in the face, thanks to the

---

96 Peritonitis in horses is commonly a result of the ingestion of sand, which attacks the
stomach wall. This was a constant threat in Egypt.

good offices of Mr Lower our troop officer, I have another one, the best I have had since joining the regiment, the only thing about her is that she kicks a bit, especially when grooming up, but I keep a pretty close eye on her and so far have got off quite lightly, and we are beginning to know one another.

It is now nearly time for evening stables so must stop, as afterwards I shall not get any time for writing, as I am grub orderly and by the time I have finished washing up the dishes, etc., the light is too bad.

Love to all, yours

Frank

---

5 July 1915

Hospital Suez

My darling Parents,

Just a line to tell you I am going along alright, but still in hospital. Hope you receive all my letters, I write about three times a week and no doubt you receive them all together. Of course there is no news to tell you, but I know you want to hear just how I am going on. Whatever you do, don't worry while I'm in hospital. I hear my horse has died, dropped down dead, I feel very upset, my luck seems quite out. All papers have been received, it does cheer me up, it takes my mind off things, as it is very slow here in hospital. Please remember me to all kind friends. So glad to hear you are both keeping so well, I do think such a lot of you all at home, and often picture it myself, and say now they are having breakfast, now dinner in the evening. Father coming home, in the garden, etc., and so you see you are all continually in my mind. Almost certain by the time you have read this letter I shall be back at camp again.

Ever your loving son

Pex

No 31 Woodland Rise, Muswell Hill, the Talleys' family home.

The Rough Riders' splendid pre-war slate blue and purple lancer uniform; these were packed away in 1914.

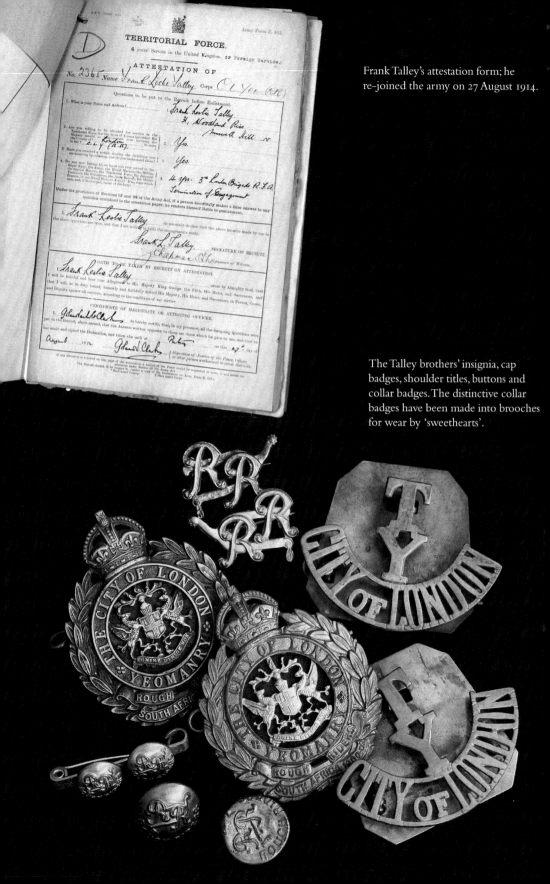

Frank Talley's attestation form; he re-joined the army on 27 August 1914.

The Talley brothers' insignia, cap badges, shoulder titles, buttons and collar badges. The distinctive collar badges have been made into brooches for wear by 'sweethearts'.

1914-15

Wishing you a HAPPY
CHRISTMAS and a
PEACEFUL NEW YEAR

from

CITY OF LONDON YEOMANRY
Rough Riders   on Service.

Cover from the Rough Riders'
Diary for 1914–15, owned by one
of the Talley brothers, depicting
the typical riding order of the day.

The Rough Riders at Woodcote,
Oxfordshire, in 1914. The Talleys
joined later, and are not in this
picture.

Bacton-on-Sea, Norfolk, 1914.
This card, sent home by Frank, shows
the position of his billet (marked with
an 'X').

'The Raider'. A contemporary
postcard showing a Zeppelin
caught in a searchlight.
The Rough Riders saw the first
Zeppelin raid, and the Talleys were
concerned about the effect of the
raiders on their family at home.

Bacton Beach.

THE RAIDER
PUBLICATION SANCTIONED BY OFFICIAL PRESS BUREAU.
(Copyright)
PUBLISHING OFFICE:
39, ST. ANDREW'S HILL, E.C.

Length, 485 ft.
Breadth, 60 ft.
Tonnage, 10,900

S.S. SCOTIAN.

TO CANADA

SS *Scotian*, the troop ship that carried the Rough Riders from Avonmouth to Egypt. This card was sent home by Percy Talley.

MALTA — Marsamuscetto Landing Stage

Valetta Harbour, Malta; the Talleys were here briefly. This card,
no doubt bought from one of the 'bum-boat' vendors, was sent
home by Percy Talley.

The expectation of the British soldier. The experience was somewhat different.

Tipperary Tommy Taking Troops to Turkey

"D" Squadron. "The City of London Rough Riders"

D Squadron, Rough Riders, at the Pyramids, Egypt. The Talley brothers, both in D Squadron, must be in this photograph.

Equipment of the
Rough Riders in
Egypt: Wolseley
pattern sun helmet,
shirt sleeves and
leather bandolier.

Postcard sent home by Percy Talley
while stationed at Port Suez, Egypt.

Indian Field Service Postcard sent home by Percy from Egypt 'as a curiosity'. Such pro forma cards were a simple means of communicating with home.

Telegram sent by Percy Talley from Alexandria in May 1915, informing his parents that he and his brother had observed the battles in the Dardanelles.

Army Form A2042.

Nothing is to be written on this except the date and signature of the sender.

Sentences not required may be erased.

If anything else is added the post card will be destroyed.

I am quite well.

~~I have been admitted into hospital.~~

~~Sick~~ } and am going on well and hope to be
~~Wounded~~ } discharged soon.

~~I am being sent down to the base.~~

I have received your { letter.
{ ~~telegram.~~
{ ~~parcel.~~

Letter follows at first opportunity.

~~I have received no~~ { lately.
~~letter from you.~~ { ~~for a long time.~~

Date   **Signature.**

G. S. & Sons, Calcutta.   *Percy*

TELEGRAM
ISSUED FROM CHIEF CABLE STATION, ELECTRA HOUSE, FINSBURY PAVEMENT.
REPLIES SHOULD BE ORDERED
Via Eastern
Doubtful words should be OFFICIALLY repeated. See Rule Book.
No inquiry respecting this Telegram can be attended to without production of this Copy.
See back of form for list of Company's Stations in London

9 MAY 15

XA 290 ALEX 14 9 TW PAX EFM =

TALLEY TELCON LN =

OWING TO RUMOURS WIRING BOTH FIT BEEN

DARDANELLES NOW ALEXANDRIA = TALLEY

Mudros Harbour, Lemnos; this was the main base for attacking the peninsula.

Suvla Bay and plain from Anzac; intended as a base for further operations. Failure to take the high ground early on meant the scheme was compromised, and hard battles were fought to exploit them.

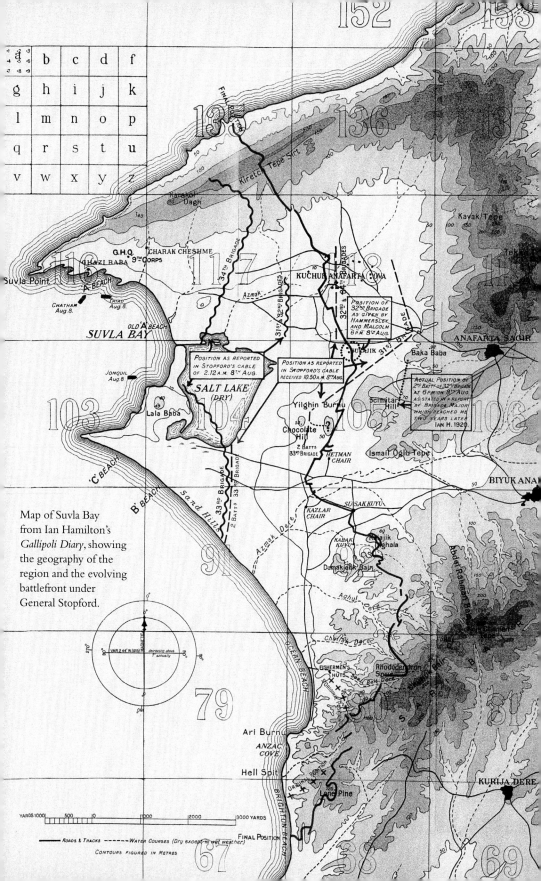

Map of Suvla Bay from Ian Hamilton's *Gallipoli Diary*, showing the geography of the region and the evolving battlefront under General Stopford.

Contemporary map showing the position of
Chocolate Hill, Hill 112 and other features of
the IX Corps' objectives on 21 August 1915.

'A' Beach, Suvla Bay, with Lala Baba to
the right, and Sari Bair in the distance.

Trench diagram showing the Ottoman
defences at Scimitar Hill and Hetman Chair.

Lala Baba: from the lee of this hill the yeomen
set off across the salt lake on 21 August 1915.

The bombardment of
Scimitar Hill, 21 August 1915.

The yeomen cross the salt
lake, 21 August 1915.

Scimitar Hill from the site
of the British positions at
Chocolate Hill; the looming
bulk of Teke Tepe ridge is in
the background.

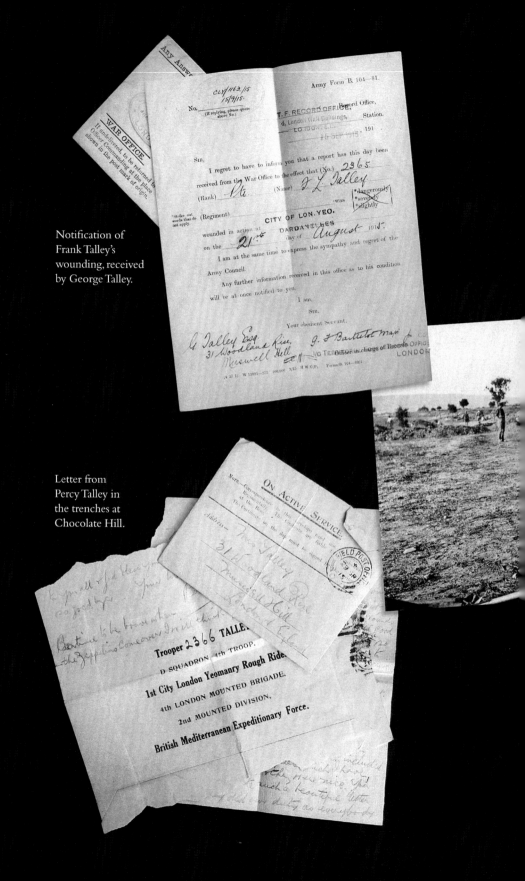

Notification of Frank Talley's wounding, received by George Talley.

Letter from Percy Talley in the trenches at Chocolate Hill.

Spotting snipers at Chocolate Hill;
the City of London Yeomanry.

The Middlesex Hussars
digging a new trench
at Chocolate Hill.

Fetching water from a well
near Chocolate Hill.

The highland barricade at Azmak Dere.

The Rough Riders' memorial in St Bartholomew the Great, in the City of London. Major Knollys, mortally wounded at Chocolate Hill, tops the list.

My dear man, were you wounded in the Big Push?
No Mum, in the Dardanelles.

'Wounded in the Dardanelles'; postcard artists make light of the suffering.

9 July 1915

Hospital Suez

My darling Parents,

Still here but getting on well think I ought to be out in a day
or so, fancy I have been in so far 3½ weeks. I hear we are moving
to Cairo, don't know if there is any truth in it. Mr Meyer sent
me quite a nice pipe and 1lb of tobacco, it came quite safely.
Hope you are all well at home we have had no letters for 12
weeks now, expect they have been delayed. The matron has lent
one of our chaps her camera and he has taken four photos of four
of us who have been together practically the whole time. I hope
they will be good, as they are funny also. One chap here is in
the H.A.C.[97] and it does seem funny to meet people out in this
distant land that you have never seen before and to learn that
they work next door to you. Am sending you a photo of our horse
lines, which is very good, hope it will go through am sending
under separate cover. Will let you know immediately I come out.

Ever your loving son

Per

10 July 1915

My dear Mother

First of all, I know you will want to hear about Percy. I am
glad to say he is getting along A.1. and is quite cheerful when
I go down to see him, generally twice a week and his leg very much
better. He certainly had as nasty a kick as one could wish for,
but fortunately no bones were broken and the skin only slightly

---

97 Honourable Artillery Company.

grazed; it has been more a question of complete rest than anything though water might have set in last Monday week. The doctor
cut the leg to get the fluid off and since then he has been
walking about a little. I shall be going down to see him this
afternoon, all being well, and hope to hear when he will be
coming back; however, there is no need to worry about him, as he
is quite OK and splendid doctors at the hospital to look after him.

Thank Father for his letter, he will be interested to hear
that when I went down to the docks last Monday for guard the
first boat I saw was the Cambria[98] sending about 16 miles of old
cable ashore that she had picked up in the Red Sea. I did not
know she had changed hands about 3 years ago, and went on board
to see the Captain, to ask him to tell you when he got back that
he had seen me but as she belonged to the E.T.C.[99] I did not do
so. I spoke to one or two of the officers on board including
the Chief Steward, who gave me a cup of tea, most acceptable,
he also sent some ashore for the other men. He about 20 years
ago, was in the Garrison Artillery – which when the Territorials
came into being were converted into the 3rd London Brigade,
R.F.A. – my old regiment[100] and the new Colonel was his Captain.

There is no news to give you, except that we are both keeping
very fit, though the life is very monotonous. We have got to
turn out to stables in a minute so will stop now.

Love to all, Yours

Frank

---

98 The Cable Ship *Cambria* was built in 1905, and worked for the Eastern Telegraph
    Company in the Red Sea during the First World War. The Talley brothers' father,
    George Talley, had worked in the submarine cable industry.

99 Eastern Telegraph Company; the ship was sold to the ETC in 1912, having originally
    been built for the Telegraph Construction and Maintenance Company Ltd.

100 Frank Talley had served with the 3rd London Brigade, Royal Field Artillery, prior to
    the war; he would later be commissioned into the brigade.

12 July 1915

Hospital Suez

My darling Parents,

Just to tell you I am getting on well and am going to ask the doctor if I can go back to camp and do light duty, I have been in here just a month. You ask if any bone was broken, well no, my leg seems quite alright. All papers have arrived with many thanks. I do not think I require anything at present. My dear Parents I was almost sorry I wrote and told you what happened, as I knew you would be so worried, but you need have no fear for me, my leg is only a trifle stiff which will no doubt pass off in time.

We hear that we have got into the narrows which is splendid news and think must be true.[101] Hope you have received all my letters with the photo by now which I thought would interest you, shall hope to send you soon as possible these that have been taken of me in the hospital. Am afraid our moving to Cairo is off, don't know what will happen to us, expect to stay here for a long time but one never knows.

Have just seen the doctor and he says I may go out tomorrow on light duty. It will be quite nice to get back to camp and see all my chums. The man riding next to me trod on the troop leaders horse and I got the kick, think I have told you everything you asked me in my last letter how I came to get kicked.

Ever your loving son

Percy

---

101 The Narrows, as their name suggests, are the narrowest part of the Dardanelles; there was no truth in the rumour that the ships had reached this point, though battle was still raging on land.

16 July 1915

4th Troop D Squadron
4th Mounted Brigade
2nd Mounted Division
City Ldn Yeo Rough Riders
Newcamp
Suez Egypt

My darling Parents,

I hope you will have received my letter of last Tuesday
telling you I was leaving hospital on that day. Am afraid
I shall not be able to ride for a little time, as my knee is
still stiff, but feel sure it is improving everyday. Will you
note the change of our address am afraid we are stuck here for
good, I feel very sick about it as I certainly want to see some
of the fun,[102] all the boys at Muswell Hill seem to be wounded.

We are hoping to have it cooler here next month so I hear,
I so hope it will be so. What do you think of the meeting
of the German bankers?[103] Of course you have read of it,
I wonder what it all means, perhaps Father will be able to
hear something.

Ever your loving son

Percy

The Abdulla cigarettes are grand quite like old times to have a
good smoke, ever the best I think and Egyptian ones are rotten.
No worrying about me.

---

102 The inaction of garrison life was telling on the Talley brothers.

103 It was reported in the Allied press on 14 July 1915 that a deputation of German bankers
had met with the Kaiser to inform him that prolonging the war into another winter
almost certainly would mean bankruptcy for Germany. He seems not to have heeded
the advice.

23 July 1915

My darling Parents,

Thank you for all your kind letters the last dated 14th was
safely received. You speak of the Stock Exchange doing a little,
which as you say the war loan[104] is the cause, I had thought of
buying a little, but not being on the spot thought I would
leave it alone.[105] They don't seem to be doing much at my place
Mr Smith and Mr Podger tell me the same, but think things must
wake up soon, at least I hope so.

Ever your loving son

Per

I think of you every time I smoke my Abdullas.

---

104 'The case for a new War Loan is overwhelming. Since the yield of the last War Loan
    ceased to cover the cost of the war, the country has been living from hand to mouth
    on money brought in by the issue of Treasury bills.' *The Spectator*, 26 June 1915.
105 Both brothers worked in the City.

24 July 1915

My dear Mother

I am glad to say your letter of the 14th turned up with this
weeks mail. Many thanks for it and the parcel on the way, they
generally take a little longer to come but will probably be
here next week. Many thanks also for all your good wishes,
I have been away for many of these days, but this I think will
be the strangest I have had.

There is no need to worry about my horse, I have got to know
her tricks now, and she has quietened down a lot and only has
occasional outbursts, which I am always ready for.

Sun Morning. I have just had a bath and done a little washing
before breakfast, but have been at a standstill for the last 10
minutes waiting for the news spirit to work, but it won't. I must
stop now, as breakfast is ready. I shall not have time to add
more after as the box is closed about 9 o'clock.

Love to you and all
Yours

Frank

30 July 1915

My darling Parents

We have been issued here with mosquito nets, life is now worth a little more.[106] The only parcel we have received to date was the one with Abdulla cigarettes and the soaps which we are very grateful for, when next sending a little of our tooth powder would be a blessing. No news here, except we have to work harder than ever, only having one night at a time in bed, it runs alternately in bed, on guard, this is of course besides the work for the day, some of us feel very tired out at times. In future I shall mention the dates of your letters, so that we can see if any go amiss, glad you are receiving all ours, am afraid at times they are very short and no news, but it tells you how we are keeping which is the chief thing. When my new horse comes I will write and tell you about him. At the present moment of writing we are both fit, I do not think May need worry about Frank at the present he is very well, please tell her from me.

Ever your loving son

Per

---

106 Two Rough Riders died from illness – enteric fever – while at Suez, caused by the heat and flies. Both men, Troopers A.C. and H.S. Herring, who were unrelated, are buried in Suez War Memorial Cemetery, Egypt, the first of the City yeomen to die in the war.

While the Egyptian garrison waited for the Ottomans to attack the canal, at Gallipoli matters had become acute. In early June, the failure of the British assaults – the Third Battle of Krithia of 4 June 1915, and the Battle of Gully Ravine some eighteen days later – meant that the commander-in-chief in the Dardanelles, General Sir Ian Hamilton, was running out of ideas. The regular 29th Division, bolstered by the Territorial 42nd (East Lancashire) Division fresh from Egypt, had again made attempts to capture the heights of Achi Baba, while there was a holding operation in the more geographically limited Anzac Sector of the peninsula. Helles seemed a tough nut to crack, and with the 'fire-eater' Hunter-Weston commanding the 29th Division being invalided home with sunstroke, options were ever more limited.

The Dardanelles adventure was becoming a major embarrassment to the government. The naval campaign, the germination of the idea, was stalled and unlikely to be resumed in the near future without the principal objective of the military campaign – the neutralisation of the threats to the navy – being enacted.

In early June, with the possibility of failure looming large, Lord Kitchener moved from his previously intransigent position – that no further reinforcements could be spared for the Dardanelles – and proposed that with Hamilton's assertion in late May and suitably bolstered by fresh troops, it should be possible to break the Ottoman stranglehold on the Allied beachheads. On 5 July, with little hope of a decisive engagement on the Western Front, Lord Kitchener agreed that five divisions should be sent to Gallipoli, and that, for a brief two-week period only, the supply of artillery shells be diverted wholly to the Dardanelles. Tellingly:

> He informed the Government at the same time that in case of necessity he would also allow Sir Ian Hamilton to call upon Sir John Maxwell, commanding the Egyptian garrison, for 15,000 British and Indian troops from Egypt. But neither of these officers was informed of his intention until the latter part of July.[ix]

This confusion would have ramifications. According to the official historian, C.F. Aspinall-Oglander:

> The arguments which preceded the despatch of 5,000 dismounted Yeomanry to Gallipoli were symptomatic of the difficulties which Sir Ian Hamilton experienced throughout almost the whole period of his command in obtaining reinforcements for the Expeditionary Force.[x]

What followed was a confusion of farcical proportions. Kitchener had promised men, but in a number of communications seemed to waiver in his resolve. Maxwell, keen to ensure that the most vital of all waterways be protected from an Ottoman threat, however remote, was reluctant to release any more 'garrison troops' from his command. And Ian Hamilton, with the offer of seemingly adequate troop numbers for the first time in his command, was equally reluctant to relinquish them. He recalled the affair in his *Gallipoli Diary*:

> In the cable telling me I would have 205,000 troops for my push, the S. of S. [Kitchener] had informed me categorically that 8,500 Yeomanry and mounted troops in Egypt ... were mine. As the present garrison of Egypt was 5,000 and as, further, there is no question of serious attack on Egypt from outside ... I therefore wired to Maxwell and asked him to organise a portion of the 8,500 mounted men, in order that, at a pinch, they might be able to come and reinforce us here.[xi]

As Hamilton would also report, Kitchener seemed to renege on his promise, when he once more cabled the commander-in-chief in the Dardanelles over the matter of the 'Egyptian Garrison troops':

> Maxwell wires that you are taking 300 officers and 5,000 men of his mounted troops. I do not quite understand why you require Egyptian Garrison troops when you have the 13th Division and Alexandria, and the 14th, the last six battalions of which are arriving in five to six days, on the Aquitania.[xii]

Yet, according to the official historian:

> When the 2nd mounted Division left England for Egypt at the end of April, Lord Kitchener intended it as a reinforcement for Gallipoli, 'if Sir Ian Hamilton needs it'. But Sir John Maxwell, commanding in Egypt, was soon urging that he could not spare it, and there for the next three months, while the Expeditionary Force was languishing for more troops, it was retained for garrison duty.[xiii]

Hamilton put an end to the debate by guaranteeing that he would not ask for the yeomen until all the other troops at his disposal were 'used up'; Kitchener relented, again asserting that Hamilton should not hesitate to ask for 'Maxwell's troops' if he required them. With Hamilton sure he would need them, Maxwell was forced to release '5,000 rifles' for service in Gallipoli as dismounted infantry. Captain Wedgwood Benn of the Middlesex Hussars, the senior regiment in the brigade, was, for one, hopeful that this would happen:

> The only relief from the tedium of our camp at Ismailia, by far the dullest spot I was in during the War, was the persistent rumour that we were soon to be moved to this theatre [Gallipoli] on which all our hopes were fixed. But month after month passed without news. It was probably with the intention of including our brigade in the first Suvla landing that at the end of July the definite announcement was made that we were, forthright, to equip as infantry.[xiv]

To make up this number of men, to the 2nd Mounted Division was added a fifth brigade, composed of the 1/1st Hertfordshire Yeomanry, and more London yeomen, the 1/2nd County of London Yeomanry (Westminster Dragoons). Orders were received by the division to prepare for its move on 2 August 1915; in just under three weeks, the Yeomen of England would see their first action in the First World War. Yet the orders to move were not without some confusion.

The Rough Riders' War Diary survives from the 1 August 1915;[xv] in the clipped language of the day, the regiment's adjutant, Lieutenant Underwood, recorded the muddle associated with the orders and counter-orders to move:

> 1st Aug 1915 SUEZ Col G.V. CLARKE DSO Comdg City Y, Capt and Adjt H.W. MALLET and Major and QM A.C. SHAWYER proceed to HQ 4th Mounted Bde ISMAILIA to receive instructions to regiments move. Returned same day arriving at 4.30
> 2 Aug 1915 SUEZ Regiment prepared to move
> 3 Aug 1915 SUEZ Regiment ready to entrain at a moments notice
> 4 Aug 1915 SUEZ Move cancelled
> 11 Aug 1915 SUEZ Instructions received. Regiment would move on the 13th inst
> 13 Aug 1915 SUEZ Regiment entrained at Suez (dismounted) for ALEXANDRIA at 9 pm

In the camp at Suez, the Rough Riders waited for their move in anticipation.

3 August 1913

My dear Father

I am sorry to be late in writing but I was suddenly called
up for dock guard so did not get time. We are living in rumours
again, for the last 4 or 5 days we have heard that there is a
move coming. Now we have heard definitely that we are to hold
ourselves in readiness to move off at any moment, so we have
packed our saddles and handed them into stores, as we shall not
be taking our horses with us at present. We believe our destination is Gallipoli, but as I say nothing is yet certain and we
may only be there for a short time, anyhow we have been told
that our last opportunity for using the Field Post Office stops
at 12 today, so I wanted you to have a line to let you know what
is happening and warn you not to worry if our letters stop for
some time. We shall of course write whenever opportunity per-
mits, and the Service P.C.s here I must stop turn out for drill.

Breakfast over, which we were in need of after an hour and
half foot drill followed by stables, so came back wet and dusty.
The last post from here is 12 o'clock today so I must finish up
as I have several things yet to do and other letters to write.

Love to all, yours

Frank

3 August 1915

My darling Parents

I suppose by this time you are back from your holidays, well
I hope you are both feeling very much better. I am glad to
say I am quite fit again. The latest news here is that we are
off to the Dardanelles in a day or two, we are not taking our
horses we have been turned into infantry, we have made all
preparations for moving we may meet the Stoecker boys[107] as this
regiment is going I hear. Think you had better address our letters with the old address, if it should be altered again will
try and let you know. You must not worry if our letters are few
and far between, as no doubt our time will be fully occupied.
Please remember me to all kind friends at Muswell Hill.

Ever your loving son

Per

Don't worry whatever you do, as we shall both turn up again.

---

107 Charles (Karl) and Max Stoecker of the 4th County of London Yeomanry
(Westminster Dragoons), a regiment that was destined to join the 2nd Mounted
Division for Gallipoli as part of the newly attached 5th Brigade.

7 August 1915

My dear Mother

There is no news to give you, I think I told you everything
in last Thursday's letter and this is only to tell you that
after all we are not going to the Dardanelles but are to
remain here. Of course we are all sorry not to be going, as we
want to do our little bit, but I know you will be glad to know
that we are not in it, anyhow at present, somehow I don't think
now we shall get another opportunity of going.

I don't remember if I mentioned in my last letter, that the
parcel of books etc., had arrived on the Sunday previous,
in the excitement of going away it is quite likely that I did,
however, many thanks for it all. This is only a line to let you
know that we are not going away so will stop now.

Love to all, yours

Frank

8 August 1915

My darling Parents

I am afraid my last letter will have given you rather a shock,
well you need not worry we are still here. Our General[108] wrote
to Sir Ian Hamilton,[109] he wrote to Lord Kitchener asking if
we might be sent to Gallipoli, but General Maxwell who is in
Command of the forces in Egypt said he would not be responsible if anything happened here if so many troops were moved.
The Colonel[110] paraded the regiment and said how sorry he was

---

108 Major General Peyton, commanding the 2nd Mounted Division.
109 Commander-in-chief of the Mediterranean Expeditionary Force, and commander of
   the Gallipoli Campaign.
110 Lieutenant Colonel Clarke.

that we were not to go, but said we must take this disappointment as we had taken the others, that in future shall not advise you of our movements until it is an accomplished fact.

All our saddles, swords, etc., had all been stored, and we had a good bye concert when our Colonel said we were really going this time. You see nothing is certain on this game. Your letters of 23 and 28 July and papers all received yesterday, think the postal department must be weary at times, when we receive about five dated five days later. You had better address letters to the new address I told you, you can still use the envelopes simply add to them, sure that will be alright.

Three of us have come out for a swim this afternoon, after we go to Suez to have dinner. I finished my swim first and am writing this letter on a brick, hence the scribble. Will you please send me £3 from my August cheque? It will come through quite safely if you send it registered. You seem to want such a lot of money here. I am keeping quite fit, also Frank.

I have got quite a nice pony in place of the one that died, I like him very much. Frank's parcel for his b'day came quite safely, and thank you so much for the Abdulla cigarettes you enclosed for me. We have just had a splendid dinner and have come on to our club to finish this letter. Two rooms, one for music and one for writing, a school by day. We must now be getting back to camp.

Ever your loving son

Pex

11 August 1915

My darling Parents

Since my last two letters, one telling you we were going to the Dardanelles, and the next cancelling it. Well it seems we might be going yet, we are getting ready to move, so perhaps I may be able to tell you something definite when I write on Saturday. We are both keeping fit, the last few days seem to have been much cooler, which makes it much easier to do ones work. This is only a note.

Ever your loving son

13 August 1915

Just a card to say we are on board, about ready to sail. We are both fit, although tired. Don't worry about us will write as soon as possible, dear.

Love to all

The next stop was Suvla Bay and their part in the ill-fated Gallipoli Campaign.

Notes

i.   George MacMunn & Cyril Falls, *Military Operations: Egypt & Palestine*, 1928, p.7.
ii.   Liman von Sanders, *Five Years in Turkey*, 1928, p.45.
iii.   A.S. Hamilton, *The City of London Yeomanry (Rough Riders)*, 1931, p.31.
iv.   A.S. Hamilton, *The City of London Yeomanry (Rough Riders)*, 1931, p.31.
v.   A.S. Hamilton, *The City of London Yeomanry (Rough Riders)*, 1931, p.31.
vi.   A.S. Hamilton, *The City of London Yeomanry (Rough Riders)*, 1931, p.32.
vii.   A.S. Hamilton, *The City of London Yeomanry (Rough Riders)*, 1931, p.37.
viii. W. Wedgwood Benn, *In the Side Shows*, 1919, p.15.
ix.   C.F. Aspinall-Oglander, *Military Operations: Gallipoli, Vol. II*, p.63.
x.   C.F. Aspinall-Oglander, *Military Operations: Gallipoli, Vol. II*, p.334.
xi.   Sir Ian Hamilton, *Gallipoli Diary, Vol. II*, 1920, p.47.
xii.   Sir Ian Hamilton, *Gallipoli Diary, Vol. II*, 1920, p.47.
xiii. C.F. Aspinall-Oglander, *Military Operations: Gallipoli, Vol. II*, p.334.
xiv.   W. Wedgwood Benn, *In the Side Shows*, 1919, p.18.
xv.   War Diary, 2nd Mounted Division, 2nd (Composite) Brigade, The National Archives, Kew.

4

The Yeomen of England

Gallipoli remains one of the most discussed campaigns of the Great War. Fought against the Ottoman Turks on their homeland over a period of just eight months from April to December 1915, the campaign was costly, with casualty rates of around 250,000 for each side.

The Allies had intended to knock the Ottomans out of the war, quickly and efficiently, by using the naval might of Britain and France in 'forcing the Dardanelles'. But this aim soon dissipated as the naval assault faltered and battle moved onto land. After the landings on 25 April 1915, the Allied forces were committed to a hard fight in which the Ottomans held the advantage. For most of the campaign, the Allies, under the command of General Sir Ian Hamilton – Britain's most experienced general not yet given a command – were left to slog it out under trying conditions, desperately seeking to break out from the small, hard-won, beachheads.

From its inception, Hamilton's force had been undermanned. And as his relationship with the British Secretary of State for War, Lord Kitchener, had been less than assertive, the supply of fresh troops to the peninsula fell foul of the pressing need for more men on the Western Front. Gallipoli remained a 'sideshow', and a costly one, but recognising how damaging a withdrawal might be to British prestige, in June the British Government's Dardanelles Committee finally committed to send fresh divisions to the peninsula.

They would not arrive before August, however, and in the meantime, despite fresh attacks in June and July, the campaign stagnated and the Allied troops were still left grimly holding on to much the same tiny parcels of land they had wrested from the determined grasp of the Ottoman Turks.

Buoyed by the promise of new troops, General Sir Ian Hamilton renewed his efforts to carry the Ottoman-held high ground and continue on to the original objectives – the capture of the coastal defences that had barred the navy from passing through in March. Taking the lead from Lieutenant General Birdwood, the Anzac commander, Hamilton proposed that the poorly held heights of Chunuk Bair – a dominating position in the Anzac Sector – should be taken in reverse. This would mean the deployment of Anzac, British and Indian troops in the complex of arid ridges and incised *nullahs* (dried up watercourses) to the north of Anzac Cove.

On 7 August, two columns would stealthily work their way up steep valleys in an attempt to get to the top of Chunuk Bair and sweep away the Ottoman defenders. Keeping the Ottomans occupied meant that the men of Anzac and Helles would once again be called to fight frontal battles against strong defensive works. There were fierce diversionary attacks by the 29th Division at Helles, and by the 1st and 2nd Australian Brigades at the heavily fortified redoubt at Lone Pine. Both actions were intended to draw enemy troops into the maelstrom, and away from the heights – the true target of the Allied offensive.

Alongside ferocious fighting to take the heights of Sari Bair, there were also new landings, full of hope, at Suvla Bay. Hamilton had been promised four new divisions by the Dardanelles Committee to reinforce his command. Yet the Allied beachheads were crowded, with little space to manoeuvre. Reinforcing either Helles or Anzac with this many men would be difficult, and could see the fresh troops frittered away with little gain. Sending them either to the head of the peninsula at Bulair – with the hopes of isolating the Ottoman garrison – or to the Asiatic shore of Anatolia, were unrealistic.

Instead, the inviting but scrub-covered plain of Suvla Bay, backed by sandy beaches and adjacent to the Anzac Sector, was the target. Formed into the IX Corps were three New Army divisions, the 10th (Irish), 11th (Northern) and 13th (Western). Attached to the new corps were the 53rd (Welsh) and 54th (East Anglian) divisions. And prised from the grasp of General Sir John Maxwell's command in Egypt, was the 2nd Mounted Division, comprising four brigades of yeomanry – men who would have to leave their horses behind, and fight on foot. An army corps of this size required a senior general to command it. With the most experienced commanders committed to the most significant front, in France and Flanders, the choice was limited. Constrained by Edwardian conceptions of seniority, only Lieutenant General Sir Frederick Stopford was available – a senior general, but one with no active experience of command.

GULF OF SAROS

134
141
133
146 132
190
161
103 156 206 241
164
282

Kiretch Tepe Sirt

165
Karakol
Dagh
•145
Ghazi Baba
•28
Azmak
Kuchuk Anafarta Ova
44•
Korgho Dere
Tekke
Tekke Tepe
278

Suvla
Point

Hill 10

SUVLA
PLAIN
Sulajik
Anafarta Sagir
†Cemetery
Windmills
114
111

SUVLA BAY
Kanli Keupru Dere

Salt Lake
[Dry]

Yilghin Burnu
Green Hill
Scimitar
Hill

△49
Lala Baba

Nibrunesi
Point

53
Chocolate
Hill

112
101
Hill 100
△
Ismail Oglu Tepe
W Hill

Biyuk
Anafarta

'C' Beach   'B' Beach

Hetman Chair

Azmak Dere

AEGEAN SEA

• Hill 60

136 146

91

Damakjelik Bair

92

△305
Koja Chemen Tepe

Agyl Dere

Bauchop's
Hill

The Farm
Hill Q

Table
Top
Chunuk Bair

204
241

Saxli Beit Dere

Rhododendron Spur

Ocean Beach

Battleship
Hill

Ari Burnu

Baby
700

Russell's
Top

ANZAC COVE

Maclagan's
Ridge

144

165

Auren Arda

Hell Spit

125•
• Lone
Pine

Kurija
Dere

94

Brighton Beach

Pine
Ridge

105

Gaba
Tepe

82   74

Though Stopford was inexperienced, he was enthusiastic. As the landings at Suvla Bay were an adjunct to the main assault of Chunuk Bair, his responsibility for securing the bay and plain as a supply base was not seen as onerous. Instead it represented a means of supporting the Anzac Sector once the heights had been captured, with the possibility reopened for the Ottoman coastal defences to be compromised and the navy to press on, once more, for Constantinople.

Perhaps for this reason Stopford was happy to let the campaign run out of steam; certainly his inexperience led to confusion. And yet compared to the tortured landscape of Anzac and the low, incised slopes of Helles, Suvla was open, constrained to the north by a sharp coastal ridge, to the south by Sari Bair range of Anzac. To the east was a ridge that connected the villages of Anafarta to the foothills of Sari Bair:

> For months the Anzac troops had looked across the Suvla Plain, surrounded on three sides by formidable hills, like an enormous amphitheatre, the salt lake glistening harshly, and the yellow aridity of the ground, which looks deceptively flat and uncomplicated, broken here and there by a few stunted olive trees. The feeling of desolation is almost tangible. There is hardly any shade, the glare from the Salt Lake assails the eyes, the ground is coarse and thirsty looking and the sentinel hills sweep in a great arc from north to south, grim, aloof and hostile, quivering in the heat.[i]

On 7 August 1915, while battle raged at Sari Bair, at Lone Pine, the Nek and Helles, the men of Stopford's command landed on the beaches at Suvla. The general had already expressed some reservations about the possibilities of untried troops landing, getting ashore and pushing on some miles over difficult ground to take a complex of hills in the face of, potentially, a determined enemy. Keen to do the right thing, he was also unduly influenced by his bullish chief of staff, Brigadier General H.L. Reed VC. Reed had seen action in France, and knew that there, artillery was king and that to undertake offensive action against prepared positions without artillery support was tantamount to madness. There were to be no guns landed in the first wave, and Reed pressed his concerns home with his chief. Yet, at Suvla, while there were no guns, equally there were no Western Front type fortifications either – and the hills were there for the taking.

Hamilton's orders to the IX Corps were simply to secure Suvla as a base: 'Your primary objective will be to secure Suvla Bay as a base for all the forces operating in the northern zone.'[111] Securing the base surely meant taking the surrounding hills, but Stopford faltered, his command fading. He tried to explain away his failure after the event, but in vague terms:

> I much regret that the force under my command has not succeeded in gain-
> ing the high ground to the east of the bay, the importance of which I fully
> recognise ... it has been a great disappointment to me that an attack I had
> fully expected would have succeeded ... turned into a defensive action.[112]

His growing indecision filtered down his command and his fresh, but admit-tedly raw, troops were squandered and their advantage of surprise evaporated under inadequate command. The possibility to carry the peninsula was lost as the newly landed troops fought against mounting odds and the debilitating difficulties of the terrain.

Stopford's resolve evaporated, as did the hopes of his commander-in-chief, who quickly disposed of the IX Corps commander and several of his subordi-nates. In the failed general's place came Major General De Lisle, commander of the 29th Division, the most experienced troops on the peninsula – men who had been committed to the Helles front since 25 April 1915.

Arriving at Suvla on 15 August, De Lisle was horrified to see the inertia and confusion of the beaches, the poverty of command and control, and the inade-quacy of the positions. His frank assessment was that the IX Corps was severely depleted, and that, day by day, the enemy facing it was growing stronger and better prepared to withhold an Allied attack. He therefore proposed that he would concentrate his action on the capture of that part of the Suvla hills that would secure the left flank of the Anzac Sector – Scimitar and W Hills – in combination with a joint Anzac, Indian and British attack led by General Godley at Hill 60, a low mound heavily defended by the Turks and threatening the security of the Anzac flank.

Slated for 21 August, the IX Corps attack would be bolstered by two brigades of the 29th Division brought from Helles, who would assault the sinuous ridge known as Scimitar Hill, and two brigades of the 11th Division, who would take the W Hills north of the Azmak Dere Valley. To the south a composite of New Army troops from the 13th Division, Gurkhas and Anzacs would assault Hill 60 under New Zealand command.

---

111 C.E. Aspinall-Oglander, *Military Operations: Gallipoli Vol. II*, p.148.
112 C.E. Aspinall-Oglander, *Military Operations: Gallipoli Vol. II*, p.299.

This was one of the largest battles of the Gallipoli Campaign, one of the most costly and, ultimately, its last offensive action. It was also this battle that would seal the fate of the commander-in-chief, Ian Hamilton, defining the enormity of the task of taking the peninsula. Much rested upon it, and into this battle the IX Corps Reserve, the 2nd Mounted Division – the Yeomen of England – were thrown, on the evening of 21 August 1915, marching across the dried out and terribly exposed salt lake of Suvla Bay directly into the throats of the enemy guns.

The topography of Suvla Bay is very different from that of the rest of the peninsula. Its spine is mountainous, created by numerous earthquakes that were as active then as they are today, and this defined the rocky difficulties of the Anzac Sector, as well as the long, rising slope of Cape Helles with Achi Baba (Alci Tepe) at its high point. But to the north of this rugged centre was the plain of Suvla, linked to the Aegean by the peculiarly arcuate bay, and to the coast of the Anzac Sector by its long curving beach. Henry Nevinson was a war correspondent in Gallipoli who could read the ground:

Inland, the plain naturally increases in area as the hills diverge towards the north-east. It is flat an open land, studded with low trees and bushes. Nearly all of the surface is waste, but small farms, surrounded by larger trees and patches of cultivation, occur here and there, as at Kazlar Chair ... and Hetman Chair about a mile north of it ('Chair' meaning meadow). The soil becomes more and more marshy as one proceeds, and in winter the region nearest the Salt Lake is waterlogged. The bush also grows more dense, but is crossed by sheep tracks, and is nowhere impenetrable.[ii]

Nevinson was aware of the importance of the surrounding hills, as well as the isolated hills that gradually coalesced with the high ground to the east that was to plague the Suvla operation. He observed what he described as a chain of hills in the bay:

The chain is now marked by a series of isolated knolls – first the low knolls around the [Nibrunesi] Point itself; then the broad-based rounded hill of Lala Baba, which rises to about 150 feet; then, beyond the southern end of the Salt Lake and a stretch of marsh and bushy plain, Yilghin Burnu (better known to us as 'Chocolate Hill', from its reddish-brown colour even before it was burnt), which is a similar but larger rounded hill, like an inverted bowl, rising about 160 feet; then beyond a brief but steepish dip or saddle, Hill 50 or 'Green Hill' (so called because the thick bush covering it was not burnt), rising to nearly equal height, but not so round or definite in shape; lastly, beyond a wide and distinctive break, the formidable mass of Ismail Oglu Tepe (known to us as 'W Hill' from the waving outline of its crest, but more officially called 'Hill 112' from its approximate height in metres.)[iii]

W Hill was a significant feature, commanding the spur of the plateau upon which the village of Biyuk Anafarta stands, and the approaches to the Sari Bair range – and the ever tantalising possibility of wresting the heights from the defenders. It was matched to the north by another significant, and easily identified feature, Scimitar Hill, east of both Chocolate and Green Hills:

> Of almost equal importance in the campaign was a rounded hill which projects sharply from the Anafarta ridge of plateau north of Ismail Oglu Tepe [W Hill]. Down the western front of this hill, which looks over the plain to the very centre of the Salt Lake, and to Suvla Bay beyond, runs a broad yellow 'blaze' of bare ground ... This 'blaze' appears from the sea to be shaped like a Gurkha's 'kukri' or an old fashioned Turkish Scimitar, and so the hill came to be called 'Scimitar Hill'. But officially it was 'Hill 70' from its height in metres, and commonly the soldiers called it 'Burnt Hill'.[iv]

To the south of these hills, across the dry valley of Azmak Dere, was another commanding feature, the spur of Damakjelik Bair and Kalajik Aghala (better known as Hill 60) beyond. Part of the foothills of the Sari Bair range, this spur blocked effective communication between Suvla Bay and the Anzac Sector and stood in the way of any chance of breaking the line by advancing up the broken topography of Sari Bair without having to take the strongly held opposing trenches of the Anzac Sector. The Battle at Lone Pine, on 6–7 August, had shown just what that would be like.

With the failure of the surprise flanking attack at Chunuk Bair, and the inertia of the Suvla landings, which served only to squander any chance there was to command the bay, Sir Ian Hamilton's opportunities for action were severely limited. Hamilton had removed the generals who had wasted opportunities, and on 18 August, at Imbros, the commander-in-chief reviewed his options for future action. He knew that the exertions of early August had severely weakened his forces, and that there was very little left in the pot. But if he could just seize 'a foothold on the high ground' then it would be possible 'to observe the drop of our shell' and 'knock out the landing places of the Turks'. Despite everything, Hamilton was still an optimist. If he could 'get the enemy on the run' he reasoned, 'with the old 29th Division and the new, keen Yeomanry on their heels, we might yet go further than we expected'.[113]

In his *Gallipoli Diary*, a memoir published in 1920, General Sir Ian Hamilton set out what he thought the purpose of the attack was on 21 August 1915:

> On the extreme right the Anzacs and Indian Brigade were to push out from Damakjelik Bair towards Hill 60. Next to them in the right centre the 11th Division was to push for the trenches at Hetman Chair. On the left centre the 29th Division were to storm the now heavily entrenched Hill 70 [Scimitar Hill]. Holding that and Ismail Oglu Tepe [W Hill] we could command the plateau between the two Anafartas; knock out the enemy's guns and observation posts commanding Suvla Bay, and should easily be able thence to work ourselves into a position whence we will enfilade the rear of the Sari Bair Ridge and begin to get a strangle grip over the Turkish communications to the southwards.[v]

With limited objectives, it all seemed perfectly reasonable.

The 2nd Mounted Division was finally woken from its canal-holding duties on 11 August, when it was confirmed that they would be moving to the Dardanelles. For the Rough Riders, this was a second chance at landing on this fateful shore, for when they stood off the coast of Cape Helles in late April, they had sincerely expected to be sent ashore. Reorganised into two squadrons, 'B' and 'D', the City of London men left Suez on the 13th, and arrived at Alexandria the following morning, ready to board the transports for the Dardanelles. With their horses left behind, the yeomen had to hand in their leather bandoliers, belts and swords. In their place was issued the usual equipment of the infantryman. The webbing straps were unfamiliar to the territorial cavalrymen, and the pouches, containing 200 rounds of .303 ammunition, were bulky:

> Infantry web equipment was served out to all ranks, and it took us some time to get accustomed to its intricacies, as not a single officer or NCO had seen anything except cavalry equipment before.[vi]

---

113 Sir Ian Hamilton, *Gallipoli Diary*, *Vol. II*, p.120.

A mass of infantry equipment was dumped in the camp; everyone was paraded and fitted with unfamiliar implements, entrenching tools, and the like.[vii]

The sword drill the Rough Riders had practised was now obsolete. The yeomen would be expected to fight with the Short Magazine Lee–Enfield rifle and bayonet alone. Equipped as an infantryman, and dressed as an infantryman, wearing broad-brimmed Wolseley sun helmet and cotton khaki drill uniform, each member of the 4th London Brigade was ready to face action for the first time.

Most men boarded HMT *Caledonia*, while a small party joined the *Knight Templar*, men who were in charge of the transport. The prosaic language of the Regimental War Diaries of the brigade's London regiments described the events:

1st County of London Yeomanry (Middlesex Hussars)
14 Aug 1915 ALEXANDRIA 9.45 am Commenced detraining at Alexandria and embarked on CALEDONIA. All carts and mules embarked on KNIGHT TEMPLAR. All transport animals were mules. Sailed in the afternoon.
1st City of London Yeomanry (Rough Riders)
14 Aug 1915 ALEXANDRIA DOCKS AT 6 am and embarked on board HMT CALADONIA [*sic*] 17 officers, 315 other ranks. Transport with 1 officer Lt E.T. PALMER and 36 other ranks embarked on HMT KNIGHT TEMPLAR sailed about 6 pm.[viii]

The *Caledonia* sailed without incident, though it might just have been a difficult crossing. That German U-boats were active in the region was underlined by the sinking of HMT *Royal Edward* close to the Greek islands on 13 August. Carrying replacement drafts for the ill-fated 29th Division, the *Royal Edward* was fortunate that the hospital ship *Soudan* was close by to pick up survivors; nevertheless, the losses were heavy. With so much shipping offshore from Gallipoli, it was feared that other troop ships could similarly be the target of German U-boats operating in the region.

Arriving at Mudros, the transport was crowded in with other ships into the tight confines of the natural harbour. Captain Wedgwood Benn of the 1st County of London Yeomanry, also on board the *Caledonia*, recorded his first impressions, boarding the ship on 13 August:

We embarked at once at Alexandria, in the Caledonia, a North Atlantic passenger ship equipped against cold rather than heat. The following day we were admitted through the boom into Lemnos harbour. Here at least we were at the 'back of the front.' Men were daily coming from and going to the war; there were hospital ships, things we had never before seen; and all around us was the parched and barren island of Mudros diapered with camps and military roads.[ix]

On board the *Caledonia* the Rough Riders and other yeomen awaited orders and received further inoculation – this time for cholera. There would be no time for recovery from any adverse reactions to the vaccine. Their final move to Gallipoli was to be made on the decks of the cruiser, HMS *Doris*, joining the other London yeomen of the 4th Brigade. Together 'they had to remain on deck, tightly packed and with barely any room to sit'.[114] At 11 p.m., the *Doris* pulled out of Mudros and set sail for Suvla. In darkness, the cruiser steamed through the night to anchor in the bay as dawn broke.

When the men had come ashore on 25 April, they had done so in open boats towed by lighters captained by midshipmen. The first troops to land on the hostile shore of Gallipoli had leapt out of the wooden-sided craft into the unknown. At Anzac, the men had beached at the cove that would bear their name forever, attempting to push up to take the very heights that men were still struggling to wrest from the grasp of the Ottoman defenders some four months later. But, in August the yeomen had the benefit of armoured craft, especially designed for such landings and the brainchild of the First Sea Lord, Lord Fisher. These 'beetles', so called due to their black colour and protruding booms, were the first real landing craft. Denied to the men on 25 April, due to wrangling within the Admiralty, they had been used for the first time on 6–7 August in the landings at Suvla. They would be used again to ferry the London yeomen ashore. The beauty of the scene that greeted them would not be lost on some:

Just before dawn on August 18th we arrived at Suvla ... a bay of exquisite beauty. Think of the most lovely part of the west coast of Scotland; make the sea perfectly calm, perfectly transparent and deep blue; imagine an ideal August day; and an invigorating breeze, and you can picture our impression of the coast of Gallipoli.[x]

114 A.S. Hamilton, *City of London Yeomanry (Rough Riders)*, 1936, p.43.

The War Diaries of the London Yeomanry recorded this momentous day with a somewhat more matter-of-fact style:

1st County of London Yeomanry (Middlesex Hussars)
18 Aug 1915 SUVLA BAY 4 am Arrived SUVLA BAY and commenced landing at 6 am; bivouacked by 9 am. Camp under shellfire but no casualties, men commenced to dig themselves in. (There was a lack of entrenching tools owing to these being put on a different boat to troops)

1st City of London Yeomanry (Rough Riders)
18 Aug 1915 SUVLA BAY Landed at SUVLA BAY about 9.30 am, unmolested, shelled soon afterwards, no casualties.

3rd County of London Yeomanry (Sharp Shooters)
18 Aug 1915 SUVLA BAY Arrived in Suvla Bay T 5.30 AM – LANDED IN BARGES without opposition from the Turkish guns, but were shelled soon after getting ashore. Dug trenches on the NORTH side of the BAY. Artillery duel between the Turks and the Battleships in the BAY during the afternoon.[xi]

With the same desultory Ottoman shellfire evident that had caused such problems to the men of the IX Corps as they had landed at Suvla on 6–7 August, there was a recognisable need to move to shelter, if random losses were not to deplete the ranks of these fresh troops. From their arrival, the men gathered on the beach and were hurried inshore to the slopes of Karakol Dagh to the north of the bay, where they were instructed to dig in:

With the whole bay overlooked and subjected to spasmodic shelling – and indeed, the same could be said of the entire Suvla Front, save only for a few blind spots which were already much over crowded in consequence – dug outs were everywhere necessary, and for want of roofing and revetting material consisted simply of open pits with the loose earth banked around.[xii]

Safely bivouacked in dugouts, the regiment awaited developments. Shellfire was constant:

The shelling was new to us. It went on more or less continuously, and we soon learned to distinguish 'Whistling Rufus', 'Asiatic Annie' (at Chanak) and the rifle and machine gun fire. All day long the battle proceeds – a fine panorama from our villa. Shells seeking the transports, bursts of shrapnel over the hidden Salt Lake, and 'whistlers' aimed at the hidden horse dugouts ... Everyone was affected in much the same way by the shells. When we had our earliest close experience of them, I think we all felt a sinking and listened very anxiously when the whistling came too near. But the depression, once the shell had exploded, was followed by a sharp rise in spirits, showing itself immediately in a desire for sheer bravado and continuously in an exhilaration when the guns were not shooting.[xiii]

At the sight of the yeomanry, Ian Hamilton was buoyed with hope: 'No end of Yeomen on the beaches: the cream of agricultural England.'[115] Despite their confidence, they were unused to their infantry role. With the exigencies of trench warfare, it was necessary to pass on the rudiments to officers and NCOs at least. The value of extemporised 'jam tin' bombs – made from tins, gun cotton, ballast and fuses – were introduced to the yeomen just a day before they needed it. And on that day, 20 August 1915, at 8 p.m., the majority of the regiment moved across the sandy beach to the protection of Lala Baba, a small knoll on the southern headland of Suvla Bay, near Nibrunesi Point. Captain O. Teichman, Medical Officer of the Worcestershire Yeomanry, surveyed the scene on the 18th:

> Looking across the Bay to the southern side, one could see the hill called Lala Baba to Point Niebruniessi [*sic*], and behind this spur could be seen numbers of our troops and guns encamped. To the south-east of our position could be seen the white coloured Salt Lake and Chocolate Hill (Yilgin Burnu) in the distance.[xiv]

The march was slow going. The Middlesex Hussars led off the brigade:

> Infinitely slowly we struggled along a road bearing around the beach to the bluff or cliff called Lala Baba, the point closest to Chocolate Hill. Very different this from our last parade ... No laughing, no talking, all awed and silent marching in a never-ending file. When we halted we lay flat for sheer rest's sake, so unused were we to the packs ... The ground at Lala

---

115 Sir Ian Hamilton, *Gallipoli Diary, Vol. II*, p.121.

Baba hid us from the guns on the Anafarta Hills, and we were thoroughly tired out when we arrived, we scarcely scratched up a protection on our allotted pitch before we sank down to rest for the night.[xv]

The Rough Riders followed on. And using their personal entrenching tools, and amongst the mass of yeomen, the Talley brothers scraped some shallow protection from shellfire and the elements.

Suddenly thrust into the front, and moved away from the order of military camps in the rear areas, the flow of correspondence from the two brothers slowed. Notepaper, once plentiful in the bazaars of Suez, was now limited, a precious commodity. All too often the inadequacies of the Field Service Postcard had to stand in for the words the two men wished to share with their beloved parents. Percy Talley took up the story from 20 August:

---

20 August 1915

Letter from the firing line
Gallipoli

My darling Parents
    I expect you will wonder why you have not received any let-
ters. I expect you will guess, I think I can tell you we are in
the firing line, you will know whereabouts. We must not tell
anything, some fellows I can hear discussing if it is worth
while writing, well this is just to tell you we are both fit.
If I cannot write you more than this shall send the printed
cards. With oceans of love to all.
    Ever your loving son

Per

Am writing this in my dugout while the enemy keep on firing.
Have met K. Stoecker,[116] Owen Minshull and others that I know.

---

116 Charles (Karl) Stoecker was serving with the 4th County of London Yeomanry, in the
    5th Brigade assigned to the division.

Percy prepared for the day's action by writing home; his brother Frank, short of writing paper but well aware of the need to keep his family informed that he was fit and well, prepared to send off a Field Service Postcard, a standard card that served only to let the recipients know that their soldier was well. Often referred to in the language of the day as 'whizz bangs', usually a nickname for a high velocity shell, but also applied to this peculiarly barren type of correspondence, a note easily dashed off before action. Frank's would be the last communication he would send home for some time:

Nothing is to be written on this side except the date and signature of the sender. Sentences not required may be erased. If anything else is added the post card will be destroyed.

I am quite well.

~~I have been admitted into hospital~~

~~Sick~~ ~~and am going on well.~~

~~Wounded~~ ~~and hope to be discharged soon.~~

~~I am being sent down to the base.~~

~~letter dated~~

~~I have received your~~ telegram "

~~parcel~~ "

Letter follows at first opportunity.

I have received no letter from you lately.

~~for a long time.~~

Signature only *Frank*

Date 20-8-15

The date 21 August was a momentous one for the yeomen, their day of destiny.

The attack began at 3 pm, following half an hour's continuous bombardment. The barrage was the best that could be mustered, but was nevertheless desultory, with little hope of seeking out the enemy's gun positions situated in the heights. With high trajectory howitzers being the only guns capable of destroying the enemy positions, and with the British guns being few in number and worn from action, the Ottoman batteries continued to fire. Naval gunfire from HMS *Swiftsure* added to the tumult, but its armour-piercing shells were ill suited to this type of work. Nevertheless, the war correspondent Ellis Ashmead-Bartlett was impressed with the work of the guns:

> Suddenly, at 2.45 pm. Every gun on land and sea, that could be brought to bear, opened up simultaneously. It was the greatest concentration of artillery fire yet seen on the Peninsula. From Chocolate Hill the scene was majestic. The enemy's positions along a mile of front seemed suddenly to go up in one vast cloud of smoke and flame, and the country behind the Anafarta Hills disappeared from view. All I could see were flames and smoke, in the midst of which trees, scrub, and huge chunks of earth were hurled into the air. It seemed as if nothing could survive such an awful pounding from so many heavy guns.[xvi]

General De Lisle's orders were for the 11th Division to capture W Hill – after having captured the Ottoman advanced trench at the area of cultivation known as Hetman Chair – while the veteran 29th Division would assault Scimitar Hill and Hill 112, the tip of the Anafarta Spur behind it. At the same time, in the Anzac Sector south of the watercourse of Azmak Dere, a composite force of British, Australian, New Zealand and Gurkha troops was to attack Hill 60 (Kalajik Aghala). Writing in 1928, the controversial correspondent Ashmead-Bartlett recalled his doubts about the attack. There was to be:

> A general attack along the whole line from Scimitar Hill to Ismail Oglu Tepe [W Hill], and from there against the Turkish trenches running across Biyuk Anafarta Valley [Azmak Dere] to Hill 60, which would be attacked by the Anzac Corps. The news filled me with consternation. To attempt further frontal attacks on Scimitar Hill and W Hill appeared to me sheer madness. The Turks had two divisions entrenched up to their necks, and if these positions could not be taken when they were held by a few battalions of gendarmes, what chance had we now?[xvii]

The poverty of the British artillery preparation soon told on the men of the 11th and 29th Divisions assaulting the strongly held hills and the open ground before them. The Ottoman forward trenches were largely untouched, and the advance trench at Hetman Chair and its long communication trench leading to W Hill was still strongly held; this would play heavily in the assault. The 11th Division attack was fiercely pressed but was met with withering fire from the Ottoman trench position at Hetman Chair. The assaulting units began to lose their way, and were repeatedly driven back by the strength of the Ottoman position. The 11th Division drive for W Hill was effectively over just two hours after its start.

To the north, the 29th Division fared little better. Close to Green Hill, the tinder dry scrubby ground was ablaze – a result of the preliminary bombardment. Here, as the assault began, men of the Royal Munster Fusiliers, attacking the Anafarta Spur, had just managed to get forward; but as more men piled to the front, the troublesome trench works at Hetman Chair once more took its toll. Casualties mounted from both the Munsters and the Lancashire Fusiliers who followed, both battalions of the 86th Brigade, 29th Division, which had lost heavily on the very first day of the landings at Cape Helles. The Ottoman front line was intact, and the wounded suffered terribly in the fires that still burned over this shell-swept landscape.

North of the 86th Brigade front, men of the Royal Inniskilling Fusiliers were to attack Scimitar Hill, backed up by other troops of the brigade as it unfolded. Tragically, this distinctive hill had once been in British hands, having been reached by men of the East Yorkshire Regiment on 8 August, but it had been given up in confusion, after the battalion was given orders to retire. Since that point it had been strongly entrenched and was a formidable objective for the Inniskillings to reach. Nevertheless, the dash of the Northern Irishmen was such that the foot of the hill was reached in the first minutes of the attack, and surging forward, they breasted the ridge top, only to be heavily enfiladed by the Turkish works on the Anafarta Spur. The casualties inflicted were appalling, and the attack was broken; the men of the Border Regiment made another attempt on the hill and were once more driven back. By 5 p.m. the attacks on the W and Scimitar Hills were effectively over.

At 3.30, while the forward brigades were making their assault and 'the attention of the enemy was engaged by these attacks',[117] the IX Corps Reserve were to move across the open plain in order to support the objectives assigned to the 29th Division and push on as far as they could go. General Peyton, once

---

117 C.F. Aspinall-Oglander, *Military Operations: Gallipoli, Vol. II*, p.341.

commander of the 2nd Mounted Division, was now in charge of the Reserve, and had selected his beloved yeomen to carry the job through.

From Lala Baba, the yeomanry led off in order, under the temporary command of Brigadier General Paul Kenna VC, crossing the Salt Lake. Captain Owen Teichman was medical officer with the 1st Worcester Yeomanry:

> At 3.10 p.m. our Division and part of the Tenth formed up behind Lala Baba, and then, crossing the ridge, commenced to descend to the Salt Lake Plain. We were in the following order: Second Brigade (Berks, Bucks and Dorset Yeomanry), Fourth Brigade (three London Yeomanry Regiments), First Brigade (Worcester, Warwick and Gloucester Yeomanry), Third Brigade (Derbyshire and two Notts Yeomanry Regiments), Fifth Brigade (Hertfordshire and Westminster Yeomanry).[xviii]

It was the crossing of the Salt Lake by the yeomen that was to impress. War correspondent H.W. Nevinson described its peculiar topography in the summer of 1915:

> The Salt Lake measures about a mile and a half at its greatest length and breadth each way, forming a kind of square with irregular sides. Its surface in summer is thinly crusted with salt deposit upon caked and fissured mud, fairly sound for walking or riding, though in places the foot sinks above the ankle, and on the south side to the knees.[xix]

Bare, the salt crystals formed from the evaporation of the lake in the summer heat, the dry lake bed shone in the sunlight and shimmered in the heat. With the yeomen in reserve, and with an absence of cover in the open Suvla Plain, there was no choice but to make the newly arrived soldiers cross the plain in full view of their enemies holding the hills beyond:

> After about half-an-hour's progress we reached the enemy's shrapnel, through which, of course, we were bound to pass if we were to attain Chocolate Hill. As each line of the division advanced into the beaten zone, the shells did their part, being timed to burst just ahead of our march. Casualties began, but our orders were strict, and forbade us to stop for anyone ... Suddenly I saw with horror my troop hit by a shell and eight men go down. The rest were splendid. They simply continued to advance in the proper formation at a walk, and waited the order, which did not come for another quarter-of-an-hour, before breaking into the double.[xx]

Starting the attack in the afternoon, the generals hoped that having crossed, the sun, now on its track to set in the west, would be shining in the eyes of the Ottoman defenders. Even these hopes would be dashed. Instead of the bright sun, there was a mysterious mist that mingled with smoke from bush fires to mask the Ottoman defenders, and make the objectives that much more difficult to make out. It was as if nature had conspired against them.

The yeomen would have to move from the cover of Lala Baba to Chocolate Hill, immediately due west of the objective, the slopes of Scimitar Hill beyond. The war correspondent, Henry Nevinson, observed the action first hand:

> The Yeomanry Division was ordered to advance from the cover of Lala Baba, where it had remained in reserve, and to take up its position under the slighter cover of Chocolate Hill. In extended order the small brigades, each numbering about 350, advanced with the steadiness and regularity of parade across the bare and fully exposed level of the Salt Lake. Some of the enemy's guns diverted their fire from Scimitar Hill and showered shrapnel over the steadily moving lines. But their regularity was exactly maintained, and owing to the accurate distance kept in the intervals the loss was small. Only too eager to reach the firing line, they forced their way through the reserves of the 11th Division around the slopes on the left side of Chocolate Hill, and plunged into the brigades at the centre of the lines, already so much confused.[xxi]

It was the crossing of the Salt Lake, in full sight of the Ottoman Turks, which stirred many observers to write in glowing terms. From his position at No 2 Outpost in the Anzac Sector, Aubrey Herbert, intelligence officer with the Anzacs, described 'an unforgettable sight':

> The dismounted Yeomanry attacked the Turks across the salt lakes of Suvla. Shrapnel burst over them continuously; above their heads there was a sea of smoke. Away to the north by Chocolate Hill fires broke out on the plain. The Yeomanry never faltered. On they came through the haze of smoke in two formations, columns and extended. Sometimes they broke into a run, but they always came on. It is difficult to describe the feelings of pride and sorrow with which we watched this advance, in which so many of our friends and relations were playing a part.[xxii]

The commander-in-chief, General Sir Ian Hamilton, also detailed the episode in some of his most descriptive prose in his *Final Despatch*:

> The advance of these English Yeomen was a sight calculated to send a thrill of pride through anyone with a drop of English blood in their veins. Such superb martial spectacles are rare in modern war. Ordinarily it would always be possible to bring up reserves under some sort of cover from shrapnel fire. Here, for a mile and a half, there was nothing to conceal a mouse, much less some of the most stalwart soldiers England has ever sent from her shores. Despite the critical events in other parts of the field, I could hardly take my glasses from the Yeomen; they moved like men on parade. Here and there a shell would take a toll of a cluster; there they lay; there was no straggling; the others moved steadily on; not a man was there who hung back or hurried.[xxiii]

John Hargrave, a witness to the battle as a member of the 32nd Field Ambulance RAMC, was scathing in his later assessment of the deployment of the yeomen after their crossing of the Salt Lake:

> The Yeomanry reached Chocolate Hill, where a hurried and almost worthless briefing took place. One brigade was to advance on Scimitar Hill, now a sinister smouldering black lump. Three brigades were to advance on Hill 112, at the tip of the Anafarta Spur. One brigade was to be held in reserve. Without more ado, and without any idea of a co-ordinated attack, the Yeomen of England 'stumbled blindly into battle'.[xxiv]

The briefing the officers received at Chocolate Hill was to the effect that: 'there was a far more formidable task than had originally anticipated. The 29th Division had failed to reach its objectives, and the Yeomanry were to try where Regular troops had failed.'[118]

The situation was challenging indeed, and there was little knowledge of what was ahead. On the left, the 2nd (South Midland) Brigade was instructed to pass through the front-line trench and attack Scimitar Hill, while on the right, the 4th (London) Brigade – with the Rough Riders at its centre – and the 1st (South Midland) Brigade would pass by Green Hill and assault Hill 112. The two other yeomanry brigades would support the attack.

---

118 C.F. Aspinall-Oglander, *Military Operations: Gallipoli, Vol. II*, p.350.

The War Diaries of the three London regiments of the 4th Brigade instructed to take Hill 112 tell the story using the barest of facts:

1/1st County of London Yeomanry (Middlesex Hussars)
21 Aug 1915 3 pm moved out with Division. The Middlesex Hussars were the leading Regiment of the Division to leave Lala Baba about 3.30 pm. We moved across on the right of the Brigade to Chocolate Hill in line of troop column. We first came under shrapnel fire at about 4.45 pm and reached Chocolate Hill at 5.15 pm. On reaching Chocolate Hill the regiment was ordered to attack round the right slope past Hill 50 [Green Hill] and if possible get a footing on Hill 112 [the tip of Anafarta Spur]. As we had not reconnoitred the ground and had no opportunity of seeing it, I ordered Capt Watson to lead my firing line consisting of two troops each of B and C Squadron, whilst I would support him with the other four troops. We found a trench running from the slopes of Hill 53 to Hill 50 and utilised this as far as possible, but found it full of Munsters and Lancashire wounded [of the 29th Division, 86th Brigade] who were crawling back that it was impossible to make any progress there, so I moved over to the slopes of Hill 50 the bush of which was then in flames. Pushing on we occupied a trench on the West slopes of Hill 105. One troop being pushed out in front and digging themselves in. I was ordered to wait here and get in touch with General W[iggin]'s Brigade [1st South Midland], who were to form on our left. A Squadron of the Warwick Yeo and Gloucester Yeo also both squadrons of the Rough Riders, they prolonged my left eventually joining with General W[iggin].[xxv]

1/1st City of London Yeomanry (Rough Riders)
21 Aug 1915 LALLA BABA [*sic*] Regiment ordered to advance with Division from LALLA BABA to CHOCOLATE HILL at 3 pm, being 2nd Regt in the advance under heavy shell fire, on arrival at CHOCOLATE HILL halted ¾ hour and called roll. Attacked position E of HILL 50 [Green Hill], which was held and improved. Casualties 7 killed 27 wounded 8 missing. Total 42.

1/3 County Of London Yeomanry (Sharp Shooters)
21 Aug 1915 LALA BABA The 2nd Mounted Division of which we formed part marched at 3.30 pm to support the attack on the Turkish

position. Heavily shelled across the open to CHOCOLATE HILL, where we deployed in the attack (2½ miles). In the attack, which followed, the Regiment formed the Reserve (third) line of the Brigade which was the RIGHT hand Brigade of the Division, and when the advance was checked, took up a position facing the RIGHT flank to counteract any counter attack. Held this position until past midnight.

The attacks were doomed to fail from the start. The objectives, such as they were, had changed. The officers in charge had received the slightest of briefings, and had therefore little chance of passing on their instructions to the men under their command:

> No one in the division had any idea of the situation in front, or what had befallen the 29th Division, or of where and when the Turks would first be encountered. Only a few senior officers, and none of the juniors, had ever seen the ground. The mist was growing thicker, scrub fires were raging, and pillars of smoke were blotting out the view. Streams of wounded were struggling back to cover. The din of battle was deafening; and daylight would only last another hour.[xxvi]

On the left of the attacking front, facing Scimitar Hill, the 2nd (South Midland) Brigade were to link with the Welshmen of the South Wales Borderers, remnants of the 29th Division (87th Brigade). At 6 p.m. the composite force struggled up the slopes of the hill, through the haze and smoke of the battlefield and managed to reach its crest – the second time that feat had been achieved that day. This achievement was soon negated, however. Commanding the top of Scimitar Hill was Hill 112 at the point of the Anafarta Spur. This strong Ottoman position remained intact, pouring enfilade fire into the British, fire that only slackened as dusk descended. In the darkness, the crest had to be given up, and the attackers once more formed a ragged line at the foothills, back where they began.

Hill 112 was the target of what remained of the 86th Brigade (29th Division). The Munsters and the Lancashire Fusiliers had already been in the thick of the action with severe losses; at 5.20 p.m., understanding that the yeomen would be pushed forward in three lines to take the hill, the 86th Brigade reserve, the 2nd Royal Fusiliers (RF), were told off to await their fellow Londoners to press forward the attack.

While their colleagues were struggling to the crest of Scimitar Hill, the fusiliers waited for the yeomen before attempting to press home their own attack. But the men of the Mounted Division failed to appear, and at 7.30 p.m., the RFs retired to Green Hill. The 4th Mounted Brigade (Rough Riders at their centre), together with the Midlanders of the 1st Brigade, had been held up. As darkness descended, they were still struggling to make headway to reach Green Hill, their progress impeded by the mass of wounded of the remnants of the 29th Division's Munster and Lancashire fusiliers. To make things worse, detachments were scattered, and took heavy casualties as they strayed into the range of the still heavily defended strongpoint of Hetman Chair, which was being assaulted, to no avail, by the 3rd (Notts & Derby) Yeomanry Brigade. And with Hill 112 still firmly in Ottoman hands, the advanced position on Scimitar Hill was untenable, the enfilade fire all too apparent.

By 9 p.m. on 21 August the battle was effectively over; at midnight, General De Lisle ordered the action to be broken off. Major General W.R. Marshall, commanding the 29th Division, was instructed to resolve the confusion. He ordered retirement to the starting position at Chocolate Hill, the recall of the yeomanry to their starting position at Lala Baba, and for carrying parties to retrieve the wounded.

Across Azmak Dere, the assault at Hill 60 by the composite force of Anzac, British and Indian troops was also a failure, with heavy loss. The last stand at Gallipoli was a failure. The Talley brothers had entered this maelstrom; both were hit on the march. Their letters in the days after the battle tell of the experience of the average trooper, each doing his duty as a 'Yeoman of England'. They had joined the Rough Riders, full of hope, in August 1914; a year into the training, their regiment was thrown against the strength of the Ottoman defences in the last battle of the Gallipoli Campaign:

> So ended the action of Scimitar Hill – at once the most costly, in proportion to its size, and the least successful of any of the Gallipoli battles. Only on the extreme right had any ground been gained, and even that small gain was recaptured by the Turks on the morning of the 22nd. The losses of the IX Corps amounted to 5,300 killed, wounded and missing out of 14,300 men who had taken part in the attack. The British troops had fought with distinguished bravery, but their task had proven impractical.[xxvii]

Percy Talley was first to write home after the battle:

22 August 1915

My darling Parents

Just a line to tell you that I expect you will have heard, that Frank is wounded, shrapnel in the chest, but he was quite cheerful when I left him to continue our advance. It has been truly an awful affair – we had to advance under an appalling fire. I was hit twice on the right arm by shrapnel but continued on. After I left Frank our advance was still awful, and how I got through this is a miracle, we had to advance from trench to trench under a heavy fire. I am thankful Frank is out of it, as he is married. I think we have to go through the same again tonight. Do think of me. I thought of you all under this terrible fire but I mean to come through. Cannot write any more, expect you will hear from Frank soon.

With love

Percy

Note from censoring officer

Frank is wounded – not seriously I think shrapnel – just about the collar bone – he came on with us, but when we got to the dressing station they kept him there. They both behaved splendidly.

R.J.B.T.

Frank was indeed wounded. The two brothers had struggled across the Salt Lake and had both been hit with shrapnel. Percy, hit in the arm, had managed to carry on. Frank, receiving a more serious wound to the chest was more debilitated. With the strict orders issued that soldiers were not to stop and aid others in the movement of the 2nd Mounted Division to the battlefront, Percy had to press on.

Neither brother would know what had happened to the other. For Frank, out of the fighting, would be the thoughts that his brother may not have come out of the continuing battle alive. For Percy, the hope that his wounded older brother would have survived his wound and blood loss as he lay in the open.

Frank would finally write home, to his wife May and his mother, some nine days after he was injured in battle. He wrote from the 3rd Australian General Hospital, which had only been set up on 8 August 1915 at Lemnos:

30 August 1915

Island of Lemnos

My dearest May

My last letter to you was dated Friday the 20th, I am sorry not to have written before, but have only just managed to borrow a couple of sheets of note paper. I could have sent one of the field service postcards but thought the news I want to tell you might have frightened you.

Now should you hear rumours that we have been in action, this time it is quite correct. After I had written you on the 20th we had orders late in the afternoon to be ready to move off at 7.30 p.m. which we were after about a 5 to 6 mile march we settled down for the night, and in the morning dug trenches for ourselves, which however were not needed.

About 3 o'clock our Colonel told us we were to be held in reserve and when the first party had taken a certain hill[119]

---

119 Hill 112.

we were to go up and relieve them. While crossing a rather long open stretch of country[120] we were very heavily shelled by the enemy. I was unfortunate enough to get hit just near the collarbone, and laid out for about 5 minutes though I never lost consciousness. So I picked myself, rifle and spade up, and made after the others to the butt of a small hill about 800 yards distant and under cover and managed to get there safely. Here I discovered that something had gone through my tunic and shirt, and there was a little blood, so was attended on the spot by the R.A.M.C. which happened to be near.

I have since been sent from pillar to post which did not improve my condition until last Friday when I was landed here, and am now under the care of the Australian R.A.M.C. and am getting very good treatment, the Doctors are splendid men the chief being, Sir Alex MacCormick[121] one of Australia's leading men.

As far as the wound goes there is absolutely nothing for you to worry about it is going on fine no bones or anything broken, simply a question of time.

Don't send any parcels here as they don't reach us in hospital but are taken and kept. Please excuse more but lack of paper forbids, but I am quite O.K. (honest Injun[122]) so please don't worry.

Love to all, yours ever

Frank

---

120 The Salt Lake.

121 Sir Alex was a distinguished surgeon. Scottish by birth, he moved to Australia to join the new medical school in the University of Sydney in 1883. He served with the New South Wales Medical Corps in the Boer War and came to the UK in 1914 to join the RAMC and serve in France with the BEF as a consulting surgeon. He was sent to Lemnos with the Australian Army Medical Corps in 1915.

122 An old term, used to emphasise the truth of something similar to 'Scout's honour'.

30 August 1915

Island of Lemnos

My dear Mother

There is not much in the way of news to give you, and I should
have written before but for lack of paper, and have only now
succeeded in borrowing a couple of sheets.

After I sent you the Field Service Card on the 20th we had
instruction to move off and the next day we received our
baptism of fire. I can only speak for myself and say that
I was early knocked out by a piece of shrapnel shell; however,
the wound was not serious and I managed to pick myself up and
go on another 500 yds or so and get under cover and get attention. Unfortunately I could not go on so had to stay behind
and after being passed from one place to another, sleeping on
the hard ground, I am safely lodged here, and on a spring bed,
so you can guess I am quite comfortable.

The wound is going on fine and ever so much better, no bones
or anything broken and except for a bit of stiffness, I feel A1.
I am sorry not to be able to give you news of Percy, though I know
he will have written should the chance permitted. The last I saw
of him was after I was hit and had covered the 500 yards already
mentioned. He was quite alright at that time so he gave me a hand,
but they had to continue to advance while I was left behind.

Please don't think of sending parcels or anything to me,
as it is quite unlikely that it would reach me, I believe all
parcels for wounded men are kept and distributed where needed.

Don't worry about me as I am quite fine, and I feel sure Percy
is too, he had all his bad luck beforehand, while I did not.

Love to all, yours ever

Frank

Official notification of Frank's wounding would be slow in coming. On 15 September 1915, the War Office sent out Army Form B.104–81 to George Talley, his father. The tone of this official pro forma was matter-of-fact. Receipt of this letter, in its brown manila 'WAR OFFICE. ON HIS MAJESTY'S SERVICE' envelope, must have been dreaded. What if things had taken a turn for the worse?

> SIR,
> I regret to have to inform you that a report has this day been received from the War Office to the effect that (No.) 2365 (Rank) Pte. (Name) F.L. Talley (Regiment) CITY OF LON. YEO. was wounded in action at DARDANELLES on the 21st day of August 1915.
> I am at the same time to express the sympathy and regret of the Army Council.
> Any further information received in this officer as to his condition will be at once notified to you.

For Percy, still at Gallipoli, the ordeal would continue. The failure of the attack on Scimitar Hill and Hill 112 on the 21st meant that on the 22nd, the 2nd Mounted Division was withdrawn. North of the Azmak Dere, the battle was over. South of it, in the Anzac Sector, the composite force struggled to wrest the summit of Hill 60 out of the grasp of the Turks. That grasp was firm. The Ottomans held on to the high ground until the evacuation.

The War Diaries of the 4th (London) Brigade outline the story of the days following. Exhausted from the assault, in the early hours of 22 August the yeomen retreated to the relative safety of Lala Baba, once more crossing the Salt Lake where the Talley brothers had received their shrapnel wounds. It was quieter this time, and the blackness of the night had closed in. Captain Wedgwood Benn of the 1st County of London Yeomanry described the relief:

> We marched back across the Salt Lake to our camp, smart sniping killing a few, but under no shell fire of any kind. We climbed the field to the place which we had started, the men lined up, orders were given to unload, ammunition was worked out the magazines and left lying where it dropped, and at dawn the whole brigade fell into their 'bivvies' and slept soundly where they lay.[xxviii]

The War Diaries of the three London Regiments of the 4th Brigade give further detail:

1/1st County of London Yeomanry (Middlesex Hussars).

22 Aug 1915 About 2.30 am on the 22nd Capt. Watson came back from my advanced troops and informed me that he was of the opinion that we might push on. I went back to the Brigadier who was in the trench 300 yards in rear and told him that I thought that by a night attack we might gain a footing on Hill 112, but that if we waited till the morning we should be decimated. While occupying the trench we were continuously under rifle fire. I sent out reconnoitring patrols to the front and to the troop I had sent out NE of us and I had two men searching in the bushes for snipers south of my position. About 1.45 am acting with orders, I sent out Lt Roller and two men to push forward and find out our best line of advance to Hill 112. About 2.15 am I received an order to retire my regiment to Lala Baba. I immediately sent out patrols and 2/Lt Benn, who was acting Adjutant, to inform the troops round me that we were ordered to retire and also to 100 men of the Border Regt who were occupying a Turkish communication trench on our right. I waited as long as possible for the return of Lt Roller and his patrol but was unable to wait for his rejoining us as I didn't wish to march my regiment across the open in daylight from Chocolate Hill to Lala Baba. We started about 2.46 and reached Lala Baba as day was breaking at about 4.45.

1/1st City of London Yeomanry (Rough Riders).

22 Aug 1915 Orders received at 2.30 am to return to bivouac behind LALLA BABA [*sic*] arriving at 4.30 AM moved out again at 8 pm to HILL 50 and went into dug outs at 10.30 pm Lt R.A.B. TROWER and 4 men of the Regiment to Hospital Ship Sick.

1/3 County Of London Yeomanry (Sharp Shooters).

22 Aug 1915 (Sunday) CHOCOLATE HILL Ordered to retire on LALA BABA at 2.30 am which we reached at 4.15 am Waited there all day. Casualties yesterday Major LLEWELLYN and 2nd Lieut de PASS wounded and 40 NCOs and men killed, wounded and missing. Marched at 8 PM for Chocolate Hill and dug ourselves in.[xxix]

The rest at Lala Baba was short lived, however. As dusk fell, the yeomanry were once again instructed to make the march back to the advanced position at Chocolate Hill, where they took stock of the situation:

1/1st County of London Yeomanry (Middlesex Hussars).

23 Aug 1915 Advanced from Lala Baba to Chocolate Hill. Received the following Chocolate Hill 23 Aug 1915: 'General Peyton wishes to convey to all ranks of the 2nd Mounted Division his high admiration of their bearing on the first occasion they took part in a general engagement. He watched with pride the steadiness of the movement from LALA BABA to CHOCOLATE HILL under heavy shrapnel fire and later the gallantry and determination displayed in the attack. He deplores the loss of our gallant comrades who fell and knows their memory will stimulate to maintain in the future the high reputation the Division has already obtained for itself. Brig. Gen. Kenna who commanded the Division has already conveyed to me his admiration of the conduct of all ranks throughout the day especially the 2nd Mtd Brigade in reaching Hill 70 in spite of heavy casualties and the loss of the Gallant Commander Lord Longford.'[123] Sgd Peyton General.

1/1st City of London Yeomanry (Rough Riders)

23 Aug 1915 CHOCOLATE HILL Regiment in reserve behind CHOCOLATE HILL Major F.R.A.N. KNOLLYS[124] wounded by shell and removed to hospital ship 2Lt G. KEKEWICH joined from SUVLA BAY.

1/3 County Of London Yeomanry (Sharp Shooters).

23 Aug 1915 CHOCOLATE HILL Shelled at intervals all day and sniped at night.

On their arrival, the yeomen of the 4th Mounted Brigade, Percy Talley amongst them, set to work improving their position as the IX Corps front moved from the offensive to the defensive. Decisions were yet to be made on what the next action would be, but in the meantime, with the Ottoman forces getting stronger by the day, it was necessary to improve the position:

---

123 Brigadier General Lord Longford personally led the 2nd (South Midland) Brigade into action against Scimitar Hill. He was posted as missing in action.

124 Major Knollys suffered a severe wound to his leg from a shell fuse; an amputation was carried out, but he died on the hospital ship. He would be the most senior officer the Rough Riders would lose during the war.

Chocolate Hill at this period was covered with low bushes, and having been temporarily occupied from time to time in emergencies was in a dreadful condition of filth and disorder. However, the troops who were now sent to hold it soon made improvements. Bushes were cut down and the ground cleared, and rows and rows of trenches and dug-outs were constructed. There was a daily shelling, and as these shells had some over the top of the hill and the shrapnel fell on the reverse slope, the beaten zone was considerably extended, in fact it seemed as if the hill was being scraped. However, as the dug outs became better constructed and the men more used to the job the casualties grew less and less numerous.[xxx]

The Rough Riders soon adapted to their new, troglodytic life:

At Chocolate Hill everybody led 'a rabbit like existence, venturing abroad only by night, but biding close to his hole by day and scuttling to it at the first note of alarm'. Blankets and some cloaks were sent up from the dump on pack mules, and much of the day was spent in sleep ... After dark, however, working parties and ration carriers left for the front line and the hill side was almost deserted.[xxxi]

Trench digging, ration parties and hard work under constant observation by enemy snipers was the lot of the yeomen. Percy Talley, still wondering about the fate of his brother since he left him on 21 August, was to take his turn in this navvies' war.

24 August 1915

My darling Parents

I wrote you the other day and got my letters posted by my
troop officer, which I hope you have received. I will repeat
what I said there. Frank was wounded rather badly, but I am
sure not seriously, of course he did not continue on. I had two
wounds both in the right arm, the first one knocked me quite
over and I hear many fellows went down with this shell. Soon
after I got another, which bruised me very badly, but I continued on to the last. It was perfect hell, we had to advance about
three miles under a most awful fire, words fail to describe it.
It was in the first three miles that I and Frank got it. After
about ½ an hour rest we continued, of course Frank was not here,
we advanced from trench to trench under a deadly fire for about
a mile, dropping down, and up again. Well, we achieved our aim
and hear every one was pleased with our work. The regulars who
watched us advance, said it was very fine for troops first time
under fire, our coolness was as fine as the regulars.

I am about as clean as this piece of paper and have grown
quite a beard. Shrapnel shells keep coming over us, the snipers
are terrible, they paint themselves green when up in trees,
or grey if they are on the ground. I was so tired as we advanced
that I actually went to sleep when lying down behind a trench,
with the bullets flying oh so close, in fact only just missing
them, it is terrible to look back on. I should think Frank would
be out of it for about 7 or 8 weeks, I am glad as he is married.
I have no more note paper left so cannot write any more letters,
but will send you the field service cards. We are in the hopes
of a big post coming in; I have not had any from home for about
two weeks. You are all continually in my thoughts, please think
of me, how nice it will be to be home once more.

My best love to you my dear parents and all.

Ever your loving son Per

I am quite well

```
Field Service Postcard
24 August 1915
I am quite well.
Percy L. Talley
```

```
Field Service Postcard
30 August 1915
I am quite well.
I received your letter dated Aug 4 and 11th
Letter follows at first opportunity.
Percy L. Talley
```

In the last days of August, and into September, the Rough Riders occupied the trenches at Chocolate Hill. This would represent the advanced line of the British at Suvla Bay; there would be no further attempts to drive the Ottomans from their ridge tops. The Regimental War Diary records the daily activity of the men, digging trenches, improving dugouts. The routine was starting to tell on the yeomen, and the combination of hard physical work, monotony of food and poverty of the water supply was to take its toll:

> Neither then nor at any time was there any shortage of food, largely because rations were indented for several days ahead and the daily decline in numbers afforded a surplus. Nor was there any real lack of variety, although the jam was always apricot, and the Maconochie ration proved too rich for stomachs after a spell of semi-liquid bully and desiccated vegetables ... As food was plentiful, so was water scarce, especially for the first few days, while the wells were being developed.[xxxii]

With water so scarce, there was little chance to wash, and the men grew beards and descended into a filthy state while in the front line. The constant buzz and drone of the flies, their numbers multiplying in the heat and fed by the dead, meant that food was contaminated, and the inability of the soldiers to have even the most basic of washes added to the inevitability of disease. The drain in manpower was continual and increasing. Daily the men were reporting sick and being sent down to the clearing station and thence on to the field ambulance.

Shelling contributed to the drain in manpower, as did the constant sniping from well-developed Ottoman posts in no-man's-land. The work of the Ottoman snipers figure in almost all accounts written from the Gallipoli battlefront. War correspondent Sydney Moseley, writing in 1916, commented:

> There has surely never been a campaign where the sniper has reaped such a harvest. Speak to any man who has taken part in the operations even for one brief hour, and he will dwell half admiringly, half wonderingly, upon the manner and means with which the enemy has potted at our men from the most unexpected places.[xxxiii]

The Rough Riders were getting wise to their attentions, however, as their War Diary recorded:

> Shelling becoming more troublesome each day, but casualties not frequent owing to improvements in dugouts and better arrangements for drawing rations and water, etc. Casualties now usually occur only from the first shell of a series, and in parties out at night from snipers.[xxxiv]

On 1 September the number of effectives stood at nine officers and 232 other ranks; just under a week later this had fallen to seven officers and 204 other ranks. This drain would continue.

Percy Talley, suffering from abdominal pain and already wounded, was living on borrowed time in the trenches of Suvla Bay; his brother Frank was well on his way to being transferred back to England.

4 September 1915

My darling Parents

I hear this morning that the wounded are being sent to England, so no doubt by this time you have seen Frank, you might let me know how he is. For myself I am quite fit and so far have dodged the shells and bullets, although at times they come far too close for my liking.[125] Would you send me some writing paper and envelopes, this is borrowed and it is also at a premium. Also some cigarettes and tobacco would be nice, if you send any only Gold Flake nothing expensive in case they get lost. It would be so nice to have a wash, my beard is coming on and is beginning to feel comfortable. The last I saw Karl Stoecker[126] he was quite fit, but was being moved from me.

Most of our work here is done at night digging trenches, etc., which is not pleasant when bullets are all around you. A job I had with nine others, going out in front of the trenches and keeping a watch was not exactly comfortable, although it is surprising how used you get to it. No doubt our casualty list will soon be in the papers and you will see for yourself our losses. How is everybody at home? I think of you so much and wonder if you are unhappy about me, well don't worry I am really quite well, please remember me to all kind friends. The money I asked you to send me has not turned up, not that I want it at the present, as there is nothing to buy[127] so don't worry about that.

Now with kind love to you all.

Ever your loving son

Pex

---

125 On this day, moving into support trenches behind the Middlesex Yeomanry, one officer was wounded and a stretcher bearer killed by a shrapnel shell.

126 Pte Charles A. Stoecker, 2nd County of London Yeomanry (Westminster Dragoons); this regiment was part of the 5th Brigade added to the 2nd Mounted Division in Egypt to make up the number of men required as reinforcements by Sir Ian Hamilton. Charles survived his experience.

127 The lack of canteens on the peninsula, where soldiers could buy simple items like stationery and condiments to help make food palatable, was a serious issue that was discussed at the highest level.

Field Service Postcard
6 September 1915
I am quite well.
Letter follows at first opportunity.
I have received no letter from you lately.
Percy L. Talley

8 September 1915

Trenches, Gallipoli

My darling Sister

Your letter of the 12th Aug I have just received and right
glad to have it this is the latest date from home, have also
received one from May[128] dated 18th please thank her for me.
Have you heard anything of Frank? Please let me know if you
can it is now 17 days since he was wounded and I have not had
a word. I suppose the letter I wrote telling of our move must
have worried you all, but you must not do so, as at the present
moment of writing I am very fit, better than I have ever been
since I left England. Life in the trenches is not over pleasant,
shells are continually coming over and you have to duck down
in your hole. You realise when a shell has just burst what
a near one you have had, you say my word I was standing up a
second or so ago just in the wake of a shell, it is all luck and
up to the present I have had it.

At night time the snipers come out and you have to walk about
head well down the whole time or else you are liable to stop
one. My two shrapnel wounds in the arm have quite disappeared
having no ill effect, I am thankful to say. Of course we have
lost a number of fellows, which makes me think and feel so sad,

128 Frank's wife.

but of course one cannot go through such a terrible ordeal
without casualties. I do hope Mother and Father are keeping
well, I do worry about them so, their last letter was from
Matlock of course letters take such a long time to come but
what can you do don't let them worry about me I don't intend to
be bowled over by a Turk. Things, although slow, are going well
with us here, and feel some things must soon end. I am my dear,
so sorry I did not think of your birthday, will you please
take the amount I told you in a letter some time back when you
mentioned about going to Weston, please do, also give my best
love to Mabel for the 10th, which I have also forgotten. It will
be grand to be home, I shall have so many exciting things to
tell you all.

I do hope we shall never have to go through such another
awful time as we did that Saturday, I am not a coward, but one
realises how terrible it all is, specially when you see your
comrades going down. That is the one thing that upsets me.
The flies in the trenches are worse than ever, suppose that
cannot be helped with all the smells caused by the dead. Please
remember me to all kind friends at Muswell Hill, I cannot write
to more than my home, I don't seem to be able to give my mind up
to it, one gets very nervy at times being bombarded and having
to sit tight all the time. I wrote Marguerite,[129] and had a reply
a week or so ago, they seem all well. I have also received
papers dated 17th and 18th August. Well old dear I think I have
told you all that I can, so will close, please give Mother and
Father a kiss from me, and many for yourself and kind love to
all and the members of the numerous families.

Ever your loving brother

Percy

---

129 One of the Belgian refugees that the Talleys looked after in London.

The number of effectives with the Rough Riders was now eight officers and 214 other ranks, through sickness, wounding and debility. Snipers had been a thorn in the side of the Allied forces at Gallipoli, and perhaps nowhere more troublesome than in the scrub-covered Suvla Plain. The Ottoman sharpshooters were audacious and determined, often establishing posts in no-man's-land – just 200–300 yards wide – to test the yeomanry front line:

> We were somewhat troubled by an enterprising Turkish post which had been pushed out to a point unpleasantly near. It was by this post, known familiarly as 'Percy', that our digging party was so badly used. The Turks in the general trench from time to time sent grenades over and fired their Maxim gun, but 'Percy' ranked as the official opposition.[xxxv]

With Percy Talley in the advanced trenches at Chocolate Hill, he was forced daily to keep his head well down to avoid the attentions of his namesake, the Ottoman sniper. Any dips in the parapet, or gathering points – like latrines – would be targeted. The yeoman brother would have to be vigilant while engaged in extending and improving his position. The Rough Riders' War Diary expresses the frustration of having to remove this nuisance once and for all:

Advance Trenches
10 Sept 1915 All men working constantly to improve parapets and continue saps.
----------06.30 One man killed behind dugouts by sniper's chance shot.
----------11.30 Two men killed by enfilade shrapnel shell while working
in trench. Sniping very troublesome from certain tree and dugout some
way in front of Turkish trench.
----------17.30 Two men crawled out of sap head to locate snipers.
One man shot and killed, the other returned with aid of covering party,
brought in body.
11 Sept 1915 At work in trenches and saps continued. Quiet day except for
the party of snipers, who have now got up sandbags round a bit of trench
running up to their tree. One man wounded when lying out with listening guard to sapping party. The stretcher bearer with him also wounded
when a mile in the rear of our trench near dressing station.
12 Sept 1915 Reconstructing traverses in all trenches and making additional ones. All men fire five rounds each during day, and attempt to drive
out sniping party.

13 Sept 1915 One sap about finished and only worked at by day. Men being rested more. Not much shelling during day.

----------19.45 Tried to turn out sniping party with one machine gun (previously sighted) and two troops, five rounds rapid, but no apparent success. And sniping continued as usual after the enemy had made a lively reply to our fire.

14 Sept 1915 02.00 Alarm from Worcester Yeo on the left, and regiment stood to arms. Very little firing. Fired from sap head at sniper's tree and dugout with rifle grenades. Sniping at night very persistent.[xxxvi]

Under constant fire from snipers, shelling and trench mortars, the Rough Riders continued with their work. It was back breaking, and the men were tired and fatigued from dysentery. Sleep was often impossible:

Three saps were being driven forward continuously under what was called the 'two hours system'. Who originated this system is undiscoverable, but it meant that in every six hours a man spent two digging, two on watch and two off duty. But as fatigues had to be performed and meals prepared, and as everybody 'stood to' morning and evening, the corporal or trooper was lucky to get a full two hours sleep at a stretch ... So tired out did the men become that at night sentries were posted in pairs to keep each other awake.[xxxvii]

Amongst this, and knowing that it was impossible to say what he really felt, Percy Talley was finding it difficult to maintain a flow of correspondence home, having to rely on 'whizz bangs' and borrowed sheets of precious paper:

Field Service Postcard
13 September 1915
I am quite well.
Letter follows at first opportunity.
I have received no letter from you lately.
Percy L. Talley

Field Service Postcard
16 September 1915
I am quite well.
I have received your letter dated 18th and 19th August.
Letter follows at first opportunity.
Percy L Talley

21 September 1915

Trenches, Gallipoli

My darling Parents,

We have just had an issue of two envelopes each man and
I have borrowed this note paper, so am able to write you a
note at last. The last letter I received from home was Aug
18th. In it you say it is the first since coming home from your
holidays. At present we are in reserve trenches, otherwise so
called rest trenches,[130] and well I can do with it too. When in
the front trenches you get practically no rest at all, it is
terrible, but I am keeping fairly fit in spite of it all.

I have not heard a word of Frank, of course I feel sure he
is alright, as I saw the wound, a nasty gash but absolutely
nothing to worry about, simply a case of waiting for new flesh
to grow. My arm is quite right now. Of course I suppose you are
all very troubled, naturally, but you must not worry if I could
only receive a letter from some of you to say you are not worrying and are all well, how happy I should be. You are both
continually in my mind night and day, but wait until I come
home, and we will have another holiday together, cheer up for
my sake I find it hard enough out here all alone.

Please remember me to all members and branches of the families,
I simply cannot write to more than you as there is such a scarcity
of paper, and no inclination. Of course we are continually under
shell fire, sometimes it seems they have forgotten all about
us, then I suppose they see a few walking about, then come the
shells one after the other, a general stampede for your dugout,
this is a very good test for your nerves, mine feel like going at
times – then again I don't care a hang, you say oh well if I get
one, I get it, and so life goes on much the same every day.

---

130 'It was soon learnt the force of the Gallipoli maxim, that the safest place was the
frontline. Spent bullets regularly came to earth in this rest area.' A.S. Hamilton, *City of
London Yeomanry (Rough Riders)*, p. 56.

I am very sorry to hear of your headaches I do hope you may soon get rid of them, do you think you could get away for a week or so rest with Father, go to a seaside place? I would be so delighted to stand expenses, to think that you and Father were accepting a short holiday from me, you could not draw mine from the bank but you could take my monthly cheques until the debt would be paid, please do this my dear parents. I do hope my letters do not take such a time to come as yours do to me. How I do wish I could pop in and see you all and have a chat, I feel quite sad when I know it is absolutely impossible, so suppose I must save everything up until I do eventually see you all.

I will try and explain a listening party's duty. We had one when building a sap, a couple of men would have to crawl out at the sap head and move along for a distance perhaps of 5 yards or so, and listen and keep watch, of course you keep absolutely flat on the ground moving along like a snake. This is done at night time; I have done it at night and day thank goodness they stopped the latter, as it was so dangerous. I had two hours of it all alone one afternoon, truly terrible, they stopped it when a few got hurt. Sniping is not so bad, we used to do it from our trench, at least not exactly ours, but occupied by another troop which looked on to the Turkish sap and also in the direction of fire from Turkish snipers, so we used to go there in turns to shoot. I am keeping this letter open until tomorrow as we are expecting a mail in. I wrote Mr Podger last on the back of one of the paper wrappers,[131] you might tell him it is very hard to write under the conditions out here and if he does not hear from me well it is simply that I have nothing to write on, or perhaps on the move we do not have much time to ourselves I often think of him and Mrs Meyer and Mr Smith, when you see them you can mention it to them if you will. The post has just arrived and not one letter from anyone, only papers dated Sept 2nd, so will close this now. With oceans of love to you all my dear ones.

Your loving son

Percy

---

131 Percy was forced to use this technique more than once. One of the wrappers is
   illustrated in the picture section.

Since the Rough Riders had come up to the front at Chocolate Hill on 20 August, they had been continuously under fire. They had been sniped at, shelled and experienced loss. They had done their best under trying conditions, and had been making the most of a difficult situation. As is so common of the British Army of the day, there was work to be done. Improvement of the trench positions, clearance of snipers and troublesome saps, construction and constant digging. The hard work and enervating conditions, the lack of suitable rest and the constant sickness was exacting. The Rough Riders' War Diary from late September makes it plain that Gallipoli was taking its toll:

2nd Mounted Division Reserve Trenches
19 Sept 1915 Regiment in reserve trenches. Strength 3 officers 201 others. Started to make dugouts for men, in place of dangerously undercut sleeping places in trenches. Worked hard until midday, not expecting any night work here. Order came to dig communication trench up to meet line at night. Rested men and worked from 19.30 to 05.30 next morning. This trench very necessary, as road now in use is well watched and constantly shelled by day.
----------17.30 Turks suddenly began heavy bombardment of British positions everywhere, especially on the left flank. Rifle fire all along line, and more bullets fall here than in front trenches. Regiment stood to arms. Our batteries, ships, replied, and soon silenced the bombardment. Gen Wiggin (GOC 1st Bde) hit just after passing end of our trench on his way to the HQ.
----------19.00 One man wounded badly, one died some hours later, getting out of the trench to go on fatigue. Sick men to Field Ambulance 3 men
20 Sept 1915 At work all day on communication trench. Sick to Field Ambulance 4 men. The daily loss of men to hospital is getting serious. The men are rather weak and diarrhoea is very prevalent. The heavy work on trench improvement wherever we go is telling on their strength and power to combat sickness.[xxxviii]

The 'daily loss of men is getting serious' – despite this growing concern, Percy Talley, still wondering about the fate of his brother, was keeping his letters home in a positive light. His time would come.

Field Service Postcard
27 September 1915
I am quite well.
Letter follows at first opportunity.
I have received no letter from you for a long time.
Percy L. Talley

28 September 1915

Trenches, Gallipoli[132]

My darling Parents,

I have just received your joint letter in one envelope acknowledging mine telling of our wounds, my word how pleased I was to have it, and to know that you had taken the news of our wounds not too seriously,[133] at least that you were in still good health. This is the only letter since Aug 19th, so some have gone astray. Please to not trouble to send me any money; perhaps you did not receive my letter, before I knew we were coming asking you to send £3 if you did, it has gone west. Don't send any papers or parcels to Frank unless you can send direct, because all parcels of wounded or killed are distributed amongst the troop, as the wounded get everything in hospital.

May sent Frank a parcel which included a pair shorts, towel and a few apples which I have, the apples I have eaten and they were nice. You are dear things to write such a beautiful letter after all we only did our duty as everybody else did, but were lucky to get through alive. I think Frank's wound is an extremely lucky one, because as I said before he only did half what I did on that day and has missed nearly six weeks of most

---

132 This letter was written on scraps of a wrapper used to mail newspapers to Percy from home (see picture section); paper was scarce in the trenches of Suvla Bay.

133 Mr and Mrs Talley would write to the local *Finchley Press* in September to announce the wounding of their two sons.

awful shell fire, which at times is terrible for the nerves and
has knocked over many of our poor chaps.

No doubt you read the account of how we came over on Aug 21st,
I believe Times Sept 4th gives a good account,[134] it was marvellous how the shells would sweep our chaps away and yet the
formation was kept and on we came. We have heard of the good
news from France,[135] and last night as far as we can judge some
of our chaps gave three cheers which was passed down the lines.
My word the Turks opened fire, and so did we, it was deafening;
talk about hell being let loose a hundred times, battleships
were firing, our land batteries, rockets were sent up, it was
most nerve racking. I think Father is a grand old man to say
he wished he was by our sides fighting I feel so proud of him,
and my dear Mother for taking the news so grandly. I cannot
tell you how the letter has bucked me up. Please thank Joe for
his card I was so pleased to have it.

I don't want to worry you but if you could send me some chocolate or toffees or some sweets, cafe au lait[136] so as I can make a
little coffee a few Gold Flake cigarettes I would be so grateful. I have written a letter to Mr Podger about 2 weeks ago,
but it is hard to write here, we are only issued with envelopes,
and am afraid I get a bit addled at times as no doubt you can
see for yourselves by my spelling.

Considering all things I am keeping pretty fit. Ask Mabel and
Wallie[137] to write me now and then as it does buck me up. I may
not be able to answer, but they will not mind that, it is lonely
here without Frank, and have not heard from him yet. How I think
of you all and the time when I shall be home again, please
continue to think of me as I know you will, please thank all

---

134 The account 'Yeomanry in Gallipoli: Glorious Baptism of Fire' was penned by the
correspondent Ellis Ashmead-Bartlett, who was on the ground to observe the attack.
'The feature of this action was a brilliant charge by the dismounted Division of Yeomanry.'
135 The Battle of Loos, the first major British offensive on the Western Front, had opened
on 25 September, though with mixed success.
136 A mixture of coffee and powdered milk popular with soldiers.
137 The Talley brothers' older siblings.

kind friends for the inquiries, Karl and Hugh[138] up to two weeks
ago were quite fit, I had a chat with them both, on Aug 21 they
both only went half way, they were lucky. Now my dear parents
I must say goodbye, with my best love and kisses to you all and
God bless you, we have just started firing again, so goodbye.
  Your loving son

Per

Continue to be brave when the Zeppelins come over,[139] I will
think of you all.

The prospect of winter in the trenches of Gallipoli was a concern. The heat of July
and August was changing, and this added to the growing gloom. There were now
storms and rainfall, and now the evident lack of water of the Suvla Plain was being
replaced by unwanted flow down the previously dry watercourses. With the yeomanry trenches being linked to these *nullahs*, it was inevitable that there was going
to be flooding to combat. Back in the advanced trenches, the Rough Riders were
making the best of a bad job. The Regimental War Diaries record their activities:

2nd Mounted Division Advance Trenches
26 Sept 1915 New position in front line joining 3rd Regt on right and
1st County Yeo[140] on our left. Right half of trenches swamped with water,
and require pumping day and night to keep passable. Four sick to Field
ambulance. Two returned from ditto.

---

138 Karl Stoecker and Hugh Minshall of the 4th County of London Yeomanry
    (Westminster Dragoons).

139 Since the first attacks on the east coast, witnessed by the Talley brothers, to the end of
    the war, Zeppelins took part in over fifty raids on Britain, causing nearly 2,000 casualties
    with some 5,000 bombs dropped. The raids caused widespread condemnation – and fear.
    For example, the *Finchley Press*, the Talleys' local newspaper, carried a banner headline on
    10 September 1915: 'The Great Air Raid 106 victims: 20 deaths'.

140 3rd County of London Yeomanry (Sharp Shooters) and 1st County of London
    Yeomanry (Middlesex Hussars), both of the 4th (London) Brigade.

----------17.00 A sudden heavy bombardment by the Turks, and regiment stood to arms

27 Sept 1915 Water rising and trench very bad. Improved by afternoon. Turks are landing broomstick bombs from a trench mortar in front and behind our lines. None in trenches.

----------19.00 Regiment had just stood to arms when loud cheering came along the line. Turks alarmed and opened fire from rifles and machine guns. Then batteries joined in and then our batteries and ships. The expenditure of ammunition by the Turks was enormous. We had no casualties and fired very little. Sick to Field Ambulance 3, returned from Field Ambulance 2.

28 Sept 1915 Heavy shelling on right end of the line. Two men, of machine gun section wounded by shrapnel from enfilade fire. Sick to Field Ambulance 5. Returned from Field Ambulance 1.

29 Sept 1915 Quiet Day. Heightened parapets with sandbags and raised floor of trench where water deepest. Officer's patrol (2/Lt Williams) sent out after dark towards Turkish trench. Sick to Field Ambulance 8, returned from Field Ambulance 2.

30 Sept 1915 10.00 Court Marshal assembled to try man asleep at his post.[141] Sick to Field Ambulance 8, wounded to Field Ambulance 1. Enfiladed by shrapnel from guns somewhere about SCIMITAR HILL also bombarded for a time with a howitzer and many bombs from trench mortar. Howitzer shells mostly failed to burst. Mortar bombs not very accurate range. Strength of effectives nine officers and 149 others.

Strafed with bombs and mortars, shelled and sniped, the yeomen had nonetheless become hardened to the rigours of front-line life. But it continued to take its toll, and the losses were becoming unmanageable. In the last week of September, some twenty-four men were evacuated to base hospital; a further thirty-nine joined them in early October. Amongst them was Percy Talley. The number of effectives in the trenches now stood at just 149.

Percy's next letter was from Alexandria. Taken out of the trenches sick, he'd passed through a chain described by the Gallipoli war correspondent Sydney Moseley in 1916:

---

141 Sentries were now posted in pairs to prevent soldiers falling asleep through tiredness. Falling asleep while on sentry duty was a serious business. The soldier concerned was found guilty and sentenced to 'penal servitude'; this was quashed when it was realised the man had been ill with dental problems. Rough justice.

The slow but sure stages from the war zone to field hospital, thence to trawler; again, on to the casualty clearing station, on to a hospital ship from Imbros to Alexandria. Thence to the comfort of a real hospital – with nurses! On to another hospital ship homewards – to hospital in London! There were very few who escaped diarrhoea.[xxxix]

15 October 1915

Left Roof
19th General Hospital[142]
Alexandria

My darling Parents

Just a line to tell you I am still in bed, feeling rather weak. The other day I went under the X-Ray and they discovered a small stone in my kidney. I am having injections to try and take it away, whatever you do don't worry, I am quite fine except for the weak state I have got into, am rather thin, but glad to say my appetite is good and we get plenty of good food, so expect I shall soon mend. How are you all at home, don't know if I shall receive letters that have been sent to the trenches, the last one I had was the one acknowledging mine telling of the wounds, I wrote you from the hospital just over a week ago, which I hope you have received. I have not heard anything of Frank yet, I left the trenches about Oct 1, was in hospital on the 5th.

Now, with oceans of love to you all.

Ever your loving son

Per

Please excuse the miserable letter. Don't worry.

---

142 There were numerous war hospitals in Alexandria.

Once again, George Talley received a manila envelope from the War Office, this time containing Army Form B.104–80A, on 25 October 1915:

SIR,

I regret to have to inform you that a report has this day been received from the War Office to the effect that (No.) 2366 (Rank) Tpr. (Name) P.L. Talley (Regiment) CITY OF LON. YEO. was admitted to 19th General Hospital Alexandria 5/10/15 suffering from debility.

Any further information received in this office as to his condition will be at once notified to you.

Percy's trials were over, and both Talley brothers had left the Dardanelles. The rest of the Rough Riders were not too far behind. They had hung on until the end of October, and had repelled at least two Ottoman attempts to test their defences at the end of the month. Their effective strength stood at just five officers and forty-six other ranks. They were evacuated to Mudros on 2 November 1915. They had 'done their bit'.

Notes

i.   Robert Rhodes James, *Gallipoli*, 1965, p.238.
ii.   H.W. Nevinson, *The Dardanelles Campaign*, 1920, p.286.
iii. H.W. Nevinson, *The Dardanelles Campaign*, 1920, pp.286–7.
iv.   H.W. Nevinson, *The Dardanelles Campaign*, 1920, p.288.
v.   Sir Ian Hamilton, *Gallipoli Diary, Vol. II*, 1920, pp.127–8.
vi.   Capt. O. Teichman, *The Diary of a Yeomanry M.O.*, 1920, p.15.
vii. Capt. W. Wedgwood Benn, *In the Side Shows*, 1919, p.18.
viii. War Diary, 2nd Mounted Division, 4th (London) Mounted Brigade, The National Archives, Kew.
ix.   Capt. W. Wedgwood Benn, *In the Side Shows*, 1919, p.19.
x.   Capt. W. Wedgwood Benn, *In the Side Shows*, 1919, p.19.
xi.   War Diary, 2nd Mounted Division, 4th (London) Mounted Brigade, The National Archives, Kew.
xii. A.S. Hamilton, *City of London Yeomanry (Rough Riders)*, 1931, p.44.
xiii. Capt. W. Wedgwood Benn, *In the Side Shows*, 1919, pp.21–2.
xiv. Capt. O. Teichman, *The Diary of a Yeomanry M.O.*, 1920, p.20.

xv.   Capt. W. Wedgwood Benn, *In the Side Shows*, 1919, pp.24–5.
xvi.   Ellis Ashmead-Bartlett, *The Uncensored Dardanelles*, 1928, p.209; Jenny
         MacLeod, in her study *Reconsidering Gallipoli* (2004), discusses the veracity of
         Ashmead-Bartlett's accounts.
xvii.   Ellis Ashmead-Bartlett, *The Uncensored Dardanelles*, 1928, p.209.
xviii.   Capt. O. Teichman, *The Diary of a Yeomanry M.O.*, 1920, p.27.
xix.   H. W. Nevinson, *The Dardanelles Campaign*, 1920, p.289.
xx.   Capt. W. Wedgwood Benn, *In the Side Shows*, 1919, p.26.
xxi.   H. W. Nevinson, *The Dardanelles Campaign*, 1920, p.345.
xxii.   Aubrey Herbert, *Mons, Anzac and Kut*, p.190.
xxiii.   *Ian Hamilton's Despatches from the Dardanelles*, 1917, p.242.
xxiv.   John Hargrave, *The Suvla Bay Landing*, p.248.
xxv.   War Diary, 2nd Mounted Division, 4th (London) Mounted Brigade, The
         National Archives, Kew.
xxvi.   C. F. Aspinall-Oglander, *Military Operations: Gallipoli, Vol. II*, 1932, p.351.
xxvii.   C. F. Aspinall-Oglander, *Military Operations: Gallipoli, Vol. II*, 1932, p.354.
xxviii. Capt. W. Wedgwood Benn, *In the Side Shows*, 1919, p.32.
xxix.   War Diary, 2nd Mounted Division, 4th (London) Mounted Brigade, The
         National Archives, Kew.
xxx.   Capt. W. Wedgwood Benn, *In the Side Shows*, 1919, p.33.
xxxi.   A. S. Hamilton, *City of London Yeomanry (Rough Riders)*, 1936, p.51.
xxxii.   A. S. Hamilton, *City of London Yeomanry (Rough Riders)*, 1936, p.52.
xxxiii. Sydney A. Moseley, *The Truth about the Dardanelles*, 1916, p.36.
xxxiv.   War Diary, 2nd Mounted Division, 4th (London) Mounted Brigade, The
         National Archives, Kew, entry for 1 September.
xxxv.   Capt. W. Wedgwood Benn, *In the Side Shows*, 1919, p.40.
xxxvi.   War Diary, 2nd Mounted Division, 4th (London) Mounted Brigade, The
         National Archives, Kew, entries for 10–14 September.
xxxvii. A. S. Hamilton, *City of London Yeomanry (Rough Riders)*, 1936, p.55.
xxxviii. War Diary, 2nd Mounted Division, 4th (London) Mounted Brigade, The
         National Archives, Kew, entries for 20–21 September.
xxxix.   Sydney A. Moseley, *The Truth about the Dardanelles*, 1916, p.153.

5

Back from Gallipoli

At home, the dreadful news from Suvla Bay was quick to sink in. The final action, the last stand at Gallipoli, was over. There was a winding down of expectations. Ellis Ashmead-Bartlett's despatch, published on 4 September 1915 in *The Times*, left no doubt:

> We have failed in the great strategic scheme of getting astride the Peninsula north of Anzac by seizing the hills around Anafarta and forcing the enemy to abandon his positions before Achi Baba and on the Kilid Bahr salient, it has certainly not been through want of trying.[i]

General Sir Ian Hamilton was in a serious situation. The offensive of 6–7 August, the assault on Sari Bair, had failed to reach the heights of the mountain and challenge the Ottoman defences on the Dardanelles. The Allied ships were still nowhere to be seen, Constantinople was still not seriously threatened and the Ottomans still held the upper hand.

The landings at Suvla Bay, with their poverty of leadership and inertia of inexperience had not even achieved its modest objectives – to create a base for supply that was secure from attack. The ring of hills that surrounded the Suvla Plain remained in Ottoman hands. Everywhere on the peninsula the axiom of 'taking the high ground' from the enemy was understood; everywhere the Ottomans held this ground, and made the Allied soldiers suffer as a consequence. The 'what ifs' of the Gallipoli Campaign are some of the greatest in military history. Yet, General Liman von Sanders, commander-in-chief of the Ottoman forces on the peninsula, was in no doubt what might have been:

The Anafarta [Suvla] landing was an enterprise planned on a grand scale, intended to open the Dardanelles to the Allies by land action while at the same time cutting the Fifth Army from its communications. If the Anafarta landing served to bring the Dardanelles Campaign to a tactical decision as desired by the British, the batteries of the fortress on the straits would have been quickly silenced as they had little ammunition. The mine-fields of the straits could then have been removed and no further difficulties would lay in the way of combined action of the victorious British Army and the Allied fleet.[ii]

Major General C.E. Callwell, Director of Military Operations and Intelligence at the War Office during the campaign, had his own view:

Whether uncontested possession of the upper crests of Sari Bair would have provided a master-key to open all gateways on the road to the Narrows must remain a matter of conjecture.[iii]

The last battle, fought on 21 August, had the air of desperation about it. All hopes of carrying the great heights and mortally wounding the Ottoman defence had now disappeared. The shrinking of the scale of objectives had become a familiar story on the peninsula. With the failure of the Battles of the Beaches on 25 April 1915 to carry the heights, the men of Gallipoli grimly held on to the territory they had wrested from an extremely well-motivated and -led enemy, an enemy that was getting stronger with each passing day, in positions that were becoming more and more impregnable.

At Helles, the successive battles in May and June, and the smaller affairs of July foundered before the modest, yet unattainable, mound of Achi Baba, a flat-topped hill that no Allied soldier would ever set foot on during the campaign. At Anzac, the extreme landscape carved from the friable sandy soils of Sari Bair was held by brave men from Australasia, India and Britain, too, who were forced to grapple a determined enemy in hard-fought battles that ultimately failed to attain the heights. The campaign had simply been bold in conception, but inadequate in execution.

The assault on Scimitar Hill and Hill 60 was therefore the death throes of the campaign. Callwell, critical of the whole affair, was particularly damning:

The later events of August hardly call for comment. The battle of the 21st, the biggest action on land of the Dardanelles adventure, partook of the nature of a forlorn hope, for it was in the main merely an attempt to improve the very unsatisfactory defensive position extending from Gaba Tepe to the Gulf of Saros which the invaders had fortuitously taken up. The plan of attack on that day was unquestionably a somewhat venturesome one, for it amounted in reality to frontal assault upon a commanding position which coincided to some extent with an amphi-theatre of high ground ... the Expeditionary Force met with defeat on the 21st. Thenceforth the Allies had to rest content with what was virtu-ally a passive role, while their adversaries settled down to trench warfare and confined themselves to trying to preserve the strategical and tactical impasse that had resulted from the great August offensive.[iv]

The failure of the August offensives, the need for action on the Western Front, and the mounting political pressure meant that the affair in the Dardanelles was drawing to its conclusion. Hamilton was recalled on 16 October. General Sir Charles Monro, arriving on 30 October, made a frank assessment of future success:

On purely military grounds, therefore, in consequence of the grave daily wastage of officers and men which occurs, and owing to the lack of prospect of being able to drive the Turks from their entrenched lines, I recommend evacuation of the peninsula.[v]

The evacuation of Suvla Bay and Anzac took place on 20 December; Helles followed on 8–9 January 1916.

The yeomen, untried in battle, and the corps reserve, had arrived in the Dardanelles on 18 August and had been committed to battle just three days later, dismounted. Their brief engagement was a costly affair. The 2nd Mounted Division was severely depleted by casualties and sickness, and by the time it had been evacuated its five brigades had been reorganised and amalgamated to form two composite ones. Withdrawn to Egypt, ultimately the division would not survive its experience and was gradually dismembered, its constituent bri-gades dispersed to other duties. It was disbanded on 21 January 1916.

General Peyton, commanding the division, was quick to recognise the supreme effort of all concerned on their departure from the peninsula:

The GOC 2nd Mounted Division wishes to convey to all ranks his great appreciation of the soldier-like qualities and fortitude, which have been so markedly evidenced during the last two months in the face of heavy losses sustained in action on August 21st, followed by exposure for ten days in a cramped and crowded situation to incessant shell-fire which caused many casualties.

The Division has been called upon, whilst continually under fire and suffering from the ravages of sickness, to carry out abnormal physical and manual exertions to maintain and improve our defences.

The time has come that the troops should be withdrawn and rested, and the GOC feels sure that, when reinforcements arrive and the Brigades are reorganised, they will return to face all hardships and difficulties which the service of King and Country may demand.[vi]

While the strategic situation was still being considered in the aftermath of the failure, the personal cost and individual sacrifices were being felt across the country. Like so many other similar instances in the shires of England, the wounding of yeomen like the Talley brothers on 21 August was enough to make the local newspapers. The local *Finchley Press* for 10 September 1915 carried the report of the action that wounded them both:

News has reached Muswell Hill that two brothers – P.L. and F.L. Talley, of 31 Woodland Rise, have been wounded at the Dardanelles. Both men joined the City of London Rough Riders, but in the recent battle, were acting as infantry. One was wounded by shrapnel in his chest and back, and the youngest received injuries to his arm. The engagement was the recent glorious charge made by the Yeomen and other regiments against the Turks.[vii]

Amongst other local people of Muswell Hill and East Finchley there were still hopes that their loved ones were safe – just as countless others had done so in similar situations up and down the country. Eleanor White wrote to the Talley family with the outside hope that her sweetheart had survived the charge:

14 September 1915

10 Park Hall Road,
East Finchley,
London, N.

Dear Madam,

Having seen in the Finchley Press of September 10th that two sons of yours have been wounded in the Yeomanry charge in Gallipoli of August 21st, I am taking the liberty of writing to you.

My sweetheart, who was in the Rough Riders, had been reported to his parents as having died on August 23rd of wounds received during this charge; and as he somehow got separated from his great friend,[143] who was also wounded, we can get no news of him. As there is a chance that your sons may have known him and have been with him, I thought I would write and ask you if you would help us, as we are all very anxious.

His name was W.J. Gibbs (Trooper), 2553, 2 Troop, B. Squadron, R.R.s, and I think he was generally known as 'Billy' or 'Gibbie'. If your sons joined at the outbreak of war, they probably joined with him at Putney, and were transferred to the 1st regiment at the same time as he. Perhaps I had better mention that as his parents do not live in London but at Bedfont, near Staines, I am making this enquiry for them.

Hoping that you will be so very kind as to help us, and trusting that your sons are well on the way to recovery,

Yours faithfully,

Eleanor K. White

Tpr. W. Fielding
C/o Post Office
Northwood
Middlesex

---

143 Trooper Walter Fielding, 2125, City of London Yeomanry (Rough Riders) survived the war.

There must have been so many similar requests for information across Britain. Though Trooper Gibbs' 'great friend', Walter Fielding, survived his experience to ultimately gain a commission in the Westmorland and Cumberland Yeomanry, Billy Gibbs had died in the service of his country. The circumstances of his death are difficult to ascertain; it is more likely that he died in the trenches of Chocolate Hill on 23 August than in the charge two days earlier. In any case, he became one of the many thousands of men who were lost in the fields of Gallipoli. He is commemorated as one of 21,000 names on the memorial to the missing of the Gallipoli Campaign, at Cape Helles – a memorial easily seen from the coast of the peninsula, and the entrance to the Dardanelles that these men fought so hard to break through.

At the time, the 'glorious charge of the Yeomen' on 21 August 1915 was to feature heavily in the press, with Ellis Ashmead-Bartlett's account in *The Times* in early September being accepted, by Percy Talley at least, as a good a description of the battle. With fellow correspondent Henry Nevinson wounded by a shrapnel ball during the action, Ashmead-Bartlett himself had been the target of artillery fire. Both had a front seat view of the attack:

YEOMEN TO THE FRONT
Orders were issued for another attack on Hill 70 by a battalion which had been held in reserve and a mounted Division in reserve behind Lala Baba. This splendid body of troops, in action for the first time, and led by men bearing some of the best known names in England, moved out from under cover and proceeded to cross the Salt Lake in open order. No sooner did they appear than the enemy concentrated a heavy shrapnel fire on the advancing lines, fully exposed as they were in the open. But the men, moving as if on parade, pressed steadily on, losing many, but never wavering.[viii]

While such reporting was reasonably contemporary with the battle, even months after the charge, in the dying days of the campaign, there was interest in the exploits of the yeomen. The public were obviously still thirsty for news about a campaign that would, it was little known, soon be over. A letter appeared in the press – syndicated by the Exchange Telegraph Company – that had been written by one of the Rough Riders to his parents at home. The account was published in the regional press on 14 December 1915, at a time when the evacuation of some 134,000 men was already in train, with the final withdrawal from Suvla and Anzac just five days later. The letter could just as well have been written by one of the Talley brothers as any other City Yeoman. The *Yorkshire Telegraph & Star*'s version was typical:

CHOCOLATE HILL

Soldier's Impressions of Gallipoli Fight

DODGING SNIPERS

Concerning the attack on Chocolate Hill, the Exchange Telegraph Company furnishes the following graphic account of the severe fighting which took place on the Gallipoli Peninsula during the month of August, which has been sent to his parents in London by a trooper of the City of London Yeomanry (Rough Riders). After giving details of the journey from Egypt, he describes how they landed on the beach at Suvla Bay, exposed to an incessant fire from the Turks, and then writes vividly of the great attack on the Turkish trenches on Saturday, 21 August. He says:-

'As we were the reserve force of the reserves, we didn't expect to play by any means a prominent part, and quite thought that the most we would get to do would be to hold the reserve trenches. But we were to learn a lot different. The programme was for the artillery to bombard the Turkish lines. The infantry were to go forward, and everything was to be a great success.

'The Turks had not got a look in, according to the programme, but unfortunately the programme was not carried through. When the infantry division moved off to the attack the Turks put shells over as fast as they could. Five or six men in the line in front of me went down like skittles, and we crossed the centre of the plain known as Salt Lake, men fell all round, principally to black shrapnel.

'As we got nearer there was rifle and machine gun fire, too, and it was from this that I got the one in my water bottle which probably saved my life. We arrived at the foot of Chocolate Hill, which afforded pretty good cover, and were congratulated by the Regulars of the 29th Division, who were watching our advance, and laid odds against us getting across.

'I suppose we rested here for about an hour, and then got the order to reform for an attack. As we stood ready to move off a shell burst overhead, killing some men, while some of the bullets hit my pack and that of the man next to me. Our next move was to get round the corner of Chocolate Hill, and as it was well covered with snipers we slipped round one at a time, at intervals. We did not lose many here.

'From there we raced forward in line and lined the parapet of a communication trench. While we lay there strings of wounded streamed through the trench below, just roughly bandaged, some groaning and moaning, and others giving us a cheery nod and wishing us luck. But it was a sight I shall never forget. From here we raced down the slope of Burnt Hill to a natural gully. When this shallow ditch was completely lined the order came to fix bayonets. The order, however, was countermanded.

'I was posted at an open spot to look out for snipers, and we had two men out as a listening patrol, who were relieved each half hour. After I had two hours on my post I got relieved. The gully was poor cover, and we lost quite a number here, but in spite of this and the continual rifle and maxim fire from all directions, a fair duty. On Sunday morning, the order came to retire to a certain line, and consolidate the position.

'It was disappointing to have to retire from the little bit of ground that had been gained at the cost of so many lives, but it was realised it could not be held against counter-attacks. We reformed, and started our march back. It was dark now, and there was no shrapnel, but the plain was well sniped. We were just about to leave the scrub, now all burnt, when my section leader asked to exchange places with the man behind him, so he could be in with his section. He did so, but immediately fell, shot in the stomach.

'Eventually, we arrived at our dug-outs, threw off our packs, which served as a pillow, and were soon asleep.

'It was the most eventful day of my life, and I should say of the majority who were there.'[ix]

'It was disappointing to retire' – but, faced with the strength of the Ottoman positions, there was little that could be done.

The Talley brothers had played their part, and had suffered the confusion and experienced the frustration. No doubt 21 August was the most momentous day of their lives. Arriving from Egypt just days before battle, they were committed to the final combat, the 'strong reserve' especially chosen to see the battle through to its conclusion and keep alive the dying embers of hope that the Gallipoli Campaign might still see some results alight.

The inadequate briefing of the brigadiers, the confusion of the troops in assaulting hills in front of them, the stalwart defence of the Ottomans, and the deepening gloom, all led to the failure of this one day's assault. The Rough Riders' training and long preparation in Britain and Egypt, their year-long journey as soldiers, had effectively ended with failure on that one night in Gallipoli, on 21 August 1915. Though they had held on, the die was cast. On both sides of Azmak Dere, in the Anzac and Suvla sectors, the inability of British, Indian or Anzac troops to carry the high ground in the largest battle so far fought was a wake-up call announcing that the strength of the assaulting troops needed to be dramatically increased. And this was not on the cards. The Gallipoli Campaign was effectively over.

Frank and Percy's brief service on the peninsula had been debilitating. Percy's evacuation from the front line in early October had seen him moved to Alexandria. In hospital he was surrounded by the many men, sick and wounded, who had escaped from the Gallipoli Campaign. He was obviously haunted by his experiences, the trauma of the trenches all too evident:

6 October 1915

19th General Hospital
Left Roof Alexandria

My darling Parents,

You will see by the address that I am in hospital, I had
rather a bad time in the trenches. My old complaint,[144] two
attacks and I have been feeling so ill for some time. Think
I am absolutely finished knocked to the wide, and I have wasted
away a lot my face and body, but you have no need to worry. I am
in good hands, they call my disease 'debility'. I am glad to be
away from it all, it was getting on my nerves. I should simply
address letters to me as

2366 Private P.L. Talley
Left Roof
19th General Hospital
Alexandria

I don't expect I shall ever (or for a long time) receive letters
that have gone to the trenches. I do hope you are all well,
don't send me anything, specially money as you do not know when
you are going to be moved. Now don't worry I am in good hands
and will write as often as possible. Shall not worry you with a
description of how I felt in the trenches with my pain.

Now with dear love

Your loving son

Percy

---

144 The recurrence of his kidney stones.

18 October 1915

19th Left Roof
General Hospital
Alexandria

My darling Parents

I have just received a bunch of old letters. Will you please
thank <u>all</u> for me. Mr Longe said he was sending some cigarettes;
well, of course, if they go to the trenches they will be divided
up amongst the boys. I am feeling much better today, although
still weak, am still having injections, it is a relief to be out
of the trenches for a time. How I do wish I could see you all at
home, you are all <u>every one of you</u> in my thoughts night and day.
One or two days here in hospital I have felt so depressed, but
I must not be so, I suppose but it is hard to be always cheerful.

I am sorry to see that Major Knollys has died, I thought he
would be in a bad way as he was such a big heavy man, he had
his leg below the knee blown off. The things I should like to
tell you but I must not on my honour. I am glad to say my face
is filling out a little, although I seem to have at times that
awful stare one gets at this game, I don't know why I write all
this but my pencil goes on writing, and it relieves my feelings,
but don't tell <u>everyone</u>. I do so worry about these awful air
raids, wondering if any of you have come to any harm, I start
thinking and come over so troubled for you all, please let me
know exactly how you all are. I am afraid this letter is a bit
depressing but I cannot help it, it is how I feel, and again
you always ask me to say exactly how I am.

Today is Tuesday and I have just finished breakfast. Have you
heard anything of Frank? He has never written to me, perhaps
he has not been able. Don't forget to thank all for writing
to me. Now I will say goodbye with all my love

Your ever loving son

Percy

Post Office Telegraphs
22 October 1915
Talley 31 Woodland Rise
Muswell Hill

Following from Alexandria small stone in kidney having infec-
tions doing well no need worry. Have written Percy.

23 October 1915

18th Gen Hospital
Alexandria

My darling Parents
  I have just received your letter of October 7th nothing
between this and September 9th. Thank you for sending the wire,
you have all been in my mind so much specially, Father for some
reason or other, I answered the wire as soon as possible. I have
also had a letter from Frank, I am so pleased he is getting so
fit again. I am going along alright, walking about a bit no need
to worry. There is not much news here in hospital, I have been
here nearly three weeks. Now with love to all and friends.
  Ever your loving son

  Percy

Have finished having injections

26 October 1915

> Block A Section 1, Room 1C
> British Red Cross Convalescent
> Hospital No 7 Montazah
> Alexandria Egypt

My darling Parents

Just a line to tell you I have been sent to a convalescent
hospital. I feel awfully weak, but am going along no need to
worry, will not write more now. Love to all.

Ever your loving son

Percy

This is about 8 miles from Alexandria

---

30 October 1915

> British Red Cross Convalescent Hospital No 7
> Block A Section 1 Room No 1C Montazah Alexandria

My darling Parents

I am just starting this letter before breakfast, and I hope
it will be more interesting than the last one. I still have the
dull feeling in my side specially when I wake up in the morning,
I don't feel over strong, but you have absolutely nothing to
worry about. Of course I don't know if the stone has gone, when
I was sent from the hospital they put on my discharge sheet from
there that I had passed it. How they know that beats me, I never
told them so, and when the doctor here spoke to me about it,
I told him that I did not tell them I had passed it; what I did

say was that I passed something in the trenches. This hospital consists of four buildings set apart from each other in most beautiful grounds. There are date trees, numerous, which you may eat to your hearts content so you can imagine me, boating, fishing bathing, none of these I have attempted.

These buildings are called blocks, the one we are in is the harem, ex Khedive Tewfik Pasha lived here. I expect you will remember he went to Constantinople last November.[145] Of course all the beautiful things in the buildings have been taken away, it certainly makes an ideal place for a convalescent hospital, nice large rooms. Tonight there is to be a band on the lawn which will certainly liven things up a little, I get very depressed at times. I met a man from the Westminster Dragoons here and I asked him if Karl Stoecker was safe[146] when he left he said yes. Mrs Stoecker might be glad to hear this, although it is a month ago. Has anything happened to Frank as regards his joining some other regiment, which I suppose they will make him do, please let me know. I do wish I could have some news from you but suppose it cannot be helped as I get moved about so. It was a relief to have Frank's letter and to know he was practically well again. I did not think his wound was so serious, it seems sometimes the slight ones are worse than the big ones. How is everybody? Please remember me to all kind friends, don't think I have any more to say, so with oceans of love to you all.

Ever your loving son

Percy

---

145 Tewfik Pasha was ruler, or Khedive, of Egypt under the British until 1892; it was his son, Abbas Hilmi Pasha, who ruled at the outbreak of war, and who was deposed in 1914 for supporting the Ottoman Empire in siding with the Central Powers.

146 Serving with the 4th County of London Yeomanry (Westminster Dragoons).

2 November 1915

British Red Cross Convalescent Hospital No 7 Montazah
Alexandria
Egypt

My darling Parents

Just a line to tell you I am going along alright. You know
when I went to see Dr Merill how my side was? It is just like
that, so stiff in the morning when I awake. I have no pain in
the stomach, I still feel so weary and not fit for much, I don't
know how long I shall be kept here. How is Father I do hope he
is quite right by now, I do hope you are keeping fit as well no
more rheumatism. For Xmas will you please give all the children the same as last year from me and if you have time to buy
Mabel and Florrie a little thing, Wallie, Tom & Charlie a few
cigarettes, Father 7/6 and yourself 7/6 and Alice 5/-. The last
letter from home was dated Oct 7th, which I received in hospital but nothing since, but suppose I must not worry as I get
moved about. The weather here still keeps very warm suppose it
is quite winter at Muswell Hill, please let me know anything
about Frank. You're not to worry about me. I hope you receive my
letters I write about every 3 days. Now with kind love to all.

Ever your loving son

Percy

4 November 1915

> British Red Cross Convalescent Hospital No 7 Montazah
> Block A·Section I Room No 1C Alexandria, Egypt

My dearie Alice [147]

Have just received your letter dated Sept 20th, also Mother
20th with packet of cigarettes, so you see how erratic the
post is. I have just sealed a letter to Mother but since then
have seen the doctor, and he sent me with a note to the chief
with the remarks I put in Mother's letter, I am going to be
X rayed again to see if any operation is necessary, if so
I think I shall get home. I do hope that letter of mine with
the officer's remarks is not going too far round, only to
friends please, You know how I hate a fuss specially when
I have only done my duty, did no better than any of the others.
No more now this was only a line to say what had happened.
With oceans of love.

Your Darling

Percy

5 November 1915

> British Red Cross Convalescent Hospital No 7 (Montazah)
> Block A Section I Room No 1C

My darling Parents

I was so pleased to receive your letter, I was afraid it would
worry you, but you must not do so any more. At present I am much
better, I only get the dull feeling in my side at times.

---

147 His sister.

They would like to operate on me but I said I would not have it done, I shall tell the doctor if they will send me to England I will have it done, as I shall never be safe, and it seems to me I shall never know when I may get another attack. I don't suppose they will agree to this, it all depends on the board but at any rate I shall put it to them and see what they say.

I had a very kind letter from Max,[148] he hoped I should soon be better and offered to send me money, he is a good boy. He says all Yeomanry are being sent to Cairo (that is wounded and sick which have come from the trenches instead of going back there) to undergo more training and then going to the front as cavalry, which front of course he does not say. You seem rather certain that I am coming home, I don't want to disappoint you but I do not think it for one moment, I wish it was only time, I could do with a rest and change but they will not send you home unless absolutely necessary, You have to go on and on till you drop. In case the censor should open this I shall put at the top my complaint, as he might think I am writing rather harshly. It was awfully good of you to send me the parcel but suppose I shall never see it, I should have enjoyed the cigarettes and chocs. What has happened to Frank? I hope he is quite himself again. Is Alice keeping well, I have not heard from her for some time, I do hope you are all safe.

You concluded I was ill, well I think I only let seven days go when I was coming from the peninsula otherwise I write most regularly, and will continue to do so. Now with dear love to all

Ever your loving son

Pex

---

148 Max Stoecker, brother of Karl, both in the Westminster Dragoons.

8 November 1915

My darling Parents

Just a line to tell you I am coming home for the operation,
when I don't know it might be in a few days, or perhaps 6 weeks.
Please do not write saying you are sorry I am having it, I feel
it is the right thing as life is not worth living at the present. Think of me when I am on the water. I feel rather nervy,
I am glad today I have put on a little flesh since I left the
peninsula so you will not, I am glad to say, see me at my worst.

I have just received after 3 months on the way Mr Meyer's
parcel of smokes which includes another pipe, 1 lb tobacco,
and 100 cigarettes. I think the regiment must have left the
peninsula, as these were untouched, as I told you all parcels
are distributed. Since my illness I have no inclination to
write to anybody except home, it is a terrible effort. How
pleased I should be to kiss all your dear faces once again,
I simply lie awake at night thinking of you all, I find it very
hard to get any sleep, and when I do go off, I am conscious of
everything that is going on.

Now with oceans of love to you all.

Ever your loving son

12 November 1915

My darling Parents,

Just a note to say I am still at the convalescent home waiting. The pains have gone but I do not feel very fit, I don't
want much to eat, when I first came in I could not get enough.
One of the boys from the regiment has been sent home, he had to
come off the peninsula sick (enteritis) so of course we had a
good yarn. Many more have been killed and wounded, about sixty
left out of 350, awful isn't it? It is certain I think that
they have come off and are now at Cairo. How is Father? I do
hope quite fit by now and Frank, what is happening? I have had
another letter from Max, he also tells me Karl is at Malta with
enteritis, the sickness is terrible. I shall have lots to tell
you all. I have been badly bitten by mosquitoes, my wrists are
badly swollen. Now I will say goodbye with dear love to all.

Ever your, loving son

Per

Loaded onto a hospital ship in November, Percy was transferred to the United
Kingdom, arriving on the 27th, his first port of call being Epsom Military
Hospital for rest and convalescence.

30 November 1915

No 5 Ward
County of London War Hospital
Epsom
Surrey

My darling Parents

Just a line to say I am in England and at the above hospital.
I have been under the XRay, and nothing is to be seen, suppose
it must have disappeared or else some mistake. I expect you will
be down to see me so will not write more. You can come anytime,
but of course don't come in the morning as everyone is busy.

Ever your loving son

Per

4 December 1915

County of London War Hospital

My darling Mother

Just a note all to yourself to thank you so much for the
sweets, it is so good of you, I will think of you every time
I take on. How kind of Mrs Stoecker to think of me. I do
hope Father, Alice arrived home safely, it was all too short.
Anybody who cares to come see me shall be delighted to see
them, but hope they won't talk about things too much. Now with
oceans of love to you all

Ever your loving son

Percy

15 December 1915

L.C.W.H

My darling Parents

Your letter I received this morning so am answering right
away. My movements are practically regular now, but the pain
is still awful, one thing to be thankful for is it does not
occur so often, bleeding practically finished. A Mrs Mottram
called to see me on Monday, she married a brother of the
Mottrams we know and lives quite close. She offered to bring me
a new laid egg, but as I told her I am not eating much, so she
made me promise I would tell her when I wanted any, it was very
kind of her.

Now I will say goodbye with oceans of love to all.

Ever your loving son

17 December 1915

My darling Parents

I have just received your letter, I have not spoken to the doctor yet I want to get quite right again in the hopes they will not want to do anything more to me, my condition is about the same. Mr Smith called yesterday & brought me a box of cigarettes, Mrs Mottram was also here, she very kindly left when he arrived. The chocs I shall want will be 8 boxes at ½lb and <u>one pound box</u> for the sister, I must give to all or none, the 2/- a lb would be enough to give for them, of course I suppose they will have gone up but never mind. I am including a box for the massage lady, she always comes to have a talk to me. About coming home, I have heard nothing more. The chocs will be nine boxes in all. If I thought I should be here for Xmas, I would get you to buy me a few boxes of Tunis dates, etc., so you had better not come down to me until the last moment before Xmas, not that I do not want to see you, but to save you expense, and if I am not coming home would sooner see you as near Xmas as possible you understand, this does not stop other members of the family. Now I will close, as lunch is just coming always with oceans of love to you all.

Ever your loving son

Per

On 10 December, with the winter conditions on the peninsula already severe, the first of the soldiers from the Anzac and Suvla sectors began an evacuation that would be complete by the 20th. The planning had been exemplary, the losses light, the ingenuity of deception complete. If only this level of detailed planning had played its part in the landings.

The men of Helles would have to wait for the new year. Some 80,000 men would have to be lifted from this fateful peninsula. When the Talley brothers read of the Allied departure, they must have wondered what it had all been for. Percy, still recovering, was shocked:

20 December 1915

My darling Parents
 Your letter just to hand, leave has I hear been stopped and to
tell the truth I do not think I am fit. I have had an awful head
today and a cold funny feeling, so do not feel like writing much,
so shall expect you Thursday. I was so looking forward to be
able to spend Xmas at home, but suppose it is all for the best
and I hope no fun will be spoilt because I am here; you go on
and not think of me during the holiday. What about the evacuation on the peninsula? It seems awful. Some of the boys from the
office are coming down on Friday to see me. Will tell you more
when you come. Now with oceans of love to all.
 Ever your loving son

Per

26 December 1915

My darling Parents
 My note, as promised to you, this is Sunday morning. Well
Xmas went off quite nicely, in fact we had quite a jolly time
dancing in the evening and a good feed, but I should have been
better pleased if I could have done it to better advantage.
Think I am going along alright, no need to worry. Mr Mottram
came to see me yesterday and brought his brother the head-
master of Caterham. Lady Lavedale, sister of Lady St Helier,
came in and gave us a packet of smokes, two packets cigarettes,
tobacco pouch (round metal), ounce of tobacco, three cigars
and a writing case. I do hope you all had a jolly time.
 Ever your loving son

Per

1 January 1916

C.L.W.H. Ward 5

My darling Parents

Just a line to wish you all the Very Best Good Wishes for a
Happy New Year. I was up till one o'clock last night, singing,
dancing, and general frivolity, feeling a trifle thick about
the head today so did not get up to breakfast as I intended
to, for the first time, but hope to do so tomorrow. Your letter
just received.

Ever your loving son

Percy

3 January 1916

My darling Parents

Your letter just to hand saying you think I am lazy, I do feel
so sorry, I wrote on Jan 1, so perhaps you have not received it.
Well I am going along alright and yet up to breakfast so you
need not worry about me. I am so pleased to hear of Frank,
I have written him a note. Please do not forget the money (£3),
as I am rather short, buying stamps and cigarettes, you cer=
tainly must not come down to me until you are quite fit, as the
weather is so awful. I am going to give this to the sister as
I see the letters have been collected. So with oceans of love.

Ever your loving son

Per

10 January 1916

County of London War Hospital Ward 5
Monday Morning

My dear Father

Just a note to say I have been up before the Major and leave
Thursday, as I told you yesterday. They will not grant me more
than 10 days furlough. My papers have been marked B division,
which means home service until I am fit.

Love to all
Your loving son

Percy

11 January 1916

County of London War Hospital
Ward 5

My darling Parents

I do hope you had a comfortable journey home, I was thinking
about you. For myself I am going along nicely, feeling the
better for being able to go out a little. I have absolutely
nothing more to tell you, we keep having a few wounded and
sick in.

Ever your loving son

Per.

Ultimately, Percy was sent to King George V Hospital, Dublin, which had opened in 1913, and despite being a military hospital has been described as having 'tall and handsome three storey ward ranges flanking a deep fore-court with a central two-storey Italianate entrance block'.[149] Percy's medical report from 26 June 1916 shows he was an invalid in Dublin for some months. The severe and debilitating conditions on the peninsula had taken its toll, but the army was not to be convinced that his military service was the cause of his condition. A medical report reviewing his case survives:

> About March 1912, suffered from pain in right loin and was ill for several months. Since that date he has had several attacks. In October 1915, sent back sick from Gallipoli to Alexandria with pain in right side, diarrhoea and micturition.[150] He states that XRay showed a stone in Right Ureter. He was invalided home to Epsom, where attempts were made to locate the stone but no stone was found. Dr Thompson Waller (London) diag-nosed stone in Right Ureter.[x]

Section 12 of this report was given over to a judgement as to whether the invalid's condition was 'caused by active service, climate, or ordinary military service'. The reporting officer makes his opinion plain: 'not so caused, began in civil life in 1912'.[xi] This statement would have repercussions. No pension would be forthcoming for disability due to war service.

---

149 Christine Casey, *Dublin: the City within the Grand and Royal Canals and the Circular Road with the Phoenix Park*, 2005, p.261.
150 Micturition is a disturbance of bladder function.

Nonetheless, a Medical Board convened on 28 June 1916 to review Percy's service and that of so many others suffering from debility, injury and sickness. The medical records, and Percy's testimony, were sufficient. The board found that though his debility was not the result of either climate or ordinary military duty, his active service under the most trying conditions had played its part. There was no mention of the wounds that he had received alongside his brother on that fateful day on 21 August 1915, wounds that had been left to heal themselves. With the judgement that his condition was 'Probably aggravated by Field Service at Gallipoli',[xii] the Medical Board ruled that 2366 Trooper Percy L. Talley be discharged 'as permanently unfit for service at home or abroad'. He was released from military service on 4 July 1916, just under two months shy of two years' military service with the Rough Riders. His brief experience at Gallipoli had been a rough ride indeed.

What of his brother? Frank Talley had been admitted to the 14th Casualty Clearing Station (a small hospital set up to provide emergency treatment and then move cases on to more permanent hospitals off the peninsula) the day after his wounding. His wounds were described as 'Gun Shot wound in the Right Arm and Right Forearm' – these were shrapnel wounds. Transferred to the hospital in Mudros, he was despatched home on the hospital ship *Itonus* on 9 September 1915, arriving in Britain some six days later, on 15 September. He would find his way through to a regional hospital in Liverpool. Mill Road Hospital was built originally as a workhouse, but from 1891 it had operated as a hospital – the Mill Road Infirmary. The flow of wounded soldiers from the front was such that general hospitals up and down the country were organised to take military personnel. (Mill Road was practically destroyed in the bombing of another war, in 1941.)

24 September 1915

Mill Road Hospital
Ward 3C Liverpool

My dear Mother

Was awfully glad to get a letter from you this morning. Many
thanks for it and the enclosure which will come in very useful.
I was sorry not to be able to write to you, but paper has been
very scarce. I lost all mine when I left the peninsula including razors brushes etc.

I don't yet know when I shall get back home, but our leave is
only seven days so for that reason I am not hurrying just for
the present to get back though I am longing to see you all again.

I too was disappointed in having to come right up here, but
suppose we have to go where there is most room, we are not in a
Military Hospital which is fortunate but in a local Infirmary
Hospital. Everything is very comfortable and the chief point the
food is a great improvement on what we have been having. On the
boat coming over we had 10 dinners out of 14 in boiled bully beef
stew. So were very fed up or under fed up with our food altogether.

After our railway journey here of 12 hours they have kept
us in bed. I had hoped to have got up today and gone out, but
unfortunately our clothes have not arrived yet from the depot,
so shall have to remain in bed.

My wound is quite healed now and have no dressing on it,
and all I want is exercise and decent grub and shall soon be
fit as ever.

Your affectionate son

Frank

27 September 1915

Mill Rd Hospital
Ward, 3C
Liverpool

My dear Mother

I have no news to give you, but I know you will be glad to have
a line, though I have nothing to report about myself yet and am
still waiting for some clothes so that I can get out a bit each
day. It is over a month since I have done anything in the walking
line, so am still a bit weak in the knees. I am longing for the
time to come when I can return to London and see you all again.

I am afraid news is very scarce with me just yet, I daresay you
have seen the good news in the papers this morning,[151] I hope it
will continue and that it may be the beginning of the end.

Now I must stop as the old Dr is coming into the ward and we
all have to be as quiet as mice, rather different to the wards
on Lemnos and the boat when we could talk and smoke.

Ever your affectionate son

Frank

---

151 No doubt reporting on the British offensive at Loos, which opened in September.

29 September 1915

Mill Rd Hospital
Ward 3C
Liverpool

My dearest Mother

Thanks for your letter received yesterday. Of course I should love to see you, if had been able to come down but I know quite well that it is impossible just now and should not think of asking you, also don't worry about writing long letter, as long as I just hear that things are all right I shall not worry, and shall always understand No News is Good News.

I managed to get my tunic and breeches back yesterday so can walk about the ward a little, it makes a nice change. The bed was getting a little monotonous especially as we could roam about the boat on our journey back, so it seemed as if we were not making any progress.

Of course for many things I am not inclined to hurry away from here, though I want to see you so much, even if I did they keep us here as long as possible & will not let us go while there is the slightest thing wrong with us.

My writing is not grand but my hands are cold, and so really is the ward, it is a long room about 80 feet long but only warmed by pipes, there are two fire places in it, but they are not allowed to be used.

By the way, there is no need for you to enclose paper in the future as I have been able to supply the shortage up here.

I did not now Knollys had died?[152] You say also I had seen him hit but that is not the case, surely I did not put that in any of my letters. I only heard about him from another RR who came back in the same boat and is now here in the next bed to myself.

---

152 Major Knollys, the most senior CLY (Rough Riders) officer to lose his life in the war, was hit by a shell while in the trenches at Chocolate Hill, and died from the amputation at home, a month later. He was 30 years of age.

He had to have his leg off on the spot, fortunately there was a dressing station handy but I should think he would be strong enough to get over it, he is only a young man, not more than a year older than myself; imagine the two poor stretcher bearers who would have to carry him a good half mile to the nearest ambulance wagon, I bet they wouldn't be sorry to get to the end of their journey.

I have heard nothing of Mr Hain for a long time, the last was that he had fallen and broken an arm or a leg, is he better yet and gone out to France?

Well I think I have exhausted all news for the time being.

Ever your affectionate son

Frank

1 October 1915

Mill Road Hospital
Ward 3C
Liverpool

My dearest Mother

At last I am up and walking about what a change, but a very nice one. I feel ever so much better for it. I only want a hair cut to feel civilised once again, if you had seen me at Lemnos with long hair and two weeks growth round my face you would not have known me, or perhaps mistaken me for the missing link.

Yesterday afternoon the Lady Mayoress of Liverpool came round, and doled out cigarettes to us three packets of Woodbines, value 4½d from her ladyship; I'd not want them, but took them for fear of hurting her ladyship's feelings. Fancy coming on a quiet visit with a brass collar of office all round her neck, I hope she doesn't come again.

We have had two concerts this week one in the building and one outside at some hall the latter I did not go to. Tonight is the free night for us to go to the Hippodrome or Olympia, while tomorrow week some of us have had an invitation to the Liverpool Yacht Club, where they give us a concert and tea so on the whole the people up here are very good to us.

Well this is rather a short letter, but I am afraid I cannot manage more just now.

Ever your affectionate son

Frank

4 October 1915

Mill Road Hospital
Ward 3C
Liverpool

My dearest Mother

I was very glad to get your note yesterday. Yesterday I went
round to Mrs Chandler's to tea, having special permission to
stay out to 6.46, had they not allowed me to do so I could not
have gone as it takes quite 40 minutes to get to their place,
just a car ride and then two stations in the underground going
under the river, perhaps I did not mention before that they
live at Birkenhead.

I also went out for a little Saturday afternoon, but it was
not very nice. They had a recruiting march here as you did
in London but the weather was rather against it being muddy
underfoot, and reminded me of the old London muddy days.

Have you had any more news from Percy yet, send it on to me
as soon as you can. I didn't tell you I had brought my watch
safely back, without the strap however, then owing to the hot
weather and perspiration got so brittle that it snapped in
half, I managed to make a substitute and after many adventures
it is still going well, it does the makers credit.

Your affectionate son

Frank

6 October 1915

Mill Rd Hospital
Ward 3C
Liverpool

My dearest Mother

Thanks for your letter of yesterday and postcard this morning.
Of course I shall not hurry to get away now, as there is I hope,
no need to fear, though I have been very unsettled as to what
I should do.

May was to have returned home today, but I had a card from
Mr Chandler this morning saying that they had persuaded her to
stay on a little longer, and also asking me round to tea also
the fellow in the next bed who is also a R.R.

Don't worry about not hearing from Percy, probably there are
letters on the way but owing to the new Bulgarian situation[153]
they are perhaps left in the van. I think it quite likely that
the regiment has been sent to some place like Lemnos for rest,
which usually consists of a deal of fatigues and guarding
prisoners, etc. so he may not have had time to do any writing
at all.

Yesterday I got my new lot of clothing back as overcoat,
shirt, socks, cardigan, etc. Please excuse more now, but I want
to send Percy another line.

Your affectionate son

Frank

---

153 The situation in the Balkans was worsening. Bulgaria, which previously maintained a
neutral stance, was now strongly aligned with the Central Powers, and had mobilised
on the pretence of 'armed neutrality'. On 22 October, Bulgaria declared war on Serbia,
and so committed the other Allies to support this beleaguered country.

9 October 1915

Mill Rd Hospital
Ward 3C
Liverpool

My dear Father

This is only just a short line as I want you to get it tomorrow.
As regards myself, I am getting along A.1 and feel ever so much
better now that I get out a little each day, though I am still
inclined to be livery? I am worse some days than others, but
still I cannot grumble after the chopping and changing about
I have had.

As I have told Mother in my last letter I am not hurrying away
from here though I shall have to go when they give the word,
we are having a pretty good clear out tomorrow so my turn will
perhaps come sooner than I expected, I don't know what time we
shall be leaving, but shall endeavour to catch the 2 o'clock
from here, due Euston 6.10 and will come down as soon as I have
landed my things at No 2.[154] Now I must close for the post

Ever your affectionate son

Frank

---

154 No 2 Onslow Villas, Frank's own home in Muswell Hill.

12 October 1915

Mill Rd Hospital
Ward 3C
Liverpool

My dear Father

It is your turn for another letter, but I don't know what to
write about as there is nothing in the way of news. I am getting along pretty well, though unfortunately I have got a bit
of a cold, probably due to the change of climate however it is
not bad, though the cough is a little irritating but I have got
some peps and they will soon put me right.

It has been a wretched wet day here rain all the time,
so have not been out. How is the garden looking, it will be a
treat to see some green grass after the sandy deserts of Egypt.
I hope you had a good crop of apples, keep one or two for me.
Now I must stop, excuse such an uninteresting epistle.

Ever your affectionate son

Frank

14 October 1915

Mill Rd Hospital
Ward 3C
Liverpool

My dearest Mother

This afternoon as it was so fine and warm I had quite a nice little outing with two other fellows, we took a tram to the pier head and then crossed the river[155] to Seacombe took another car to New Brighton and back from there by the ferry.

I think I can safely say that my stomach is settling down a bit now, it certainly is very much better than when I first came here, my cold is also much better. I am glad you have heard again from Percy and that he is all right. It is rather difficult to say what is best to do about sending out things to him, of course if they get sent back to Egypt they can get more clothing there, but on the other hand I know he did not have pants or vest on when he left and should be very glad of those garments now, even when I left the nights were quite chilly lying without blankets, though probably they may have these by now.

It is late now so I must stop for post.

Your affectionate son

Frank

---

155 The River Mersey.

15 October 1915

Mill Rd Hospital
Ward 3C
Liverpool

My dearest Father

I was surprised and glad to see a letter in your handwriting
this morning and to hear from yourself that you are getting on.
You have asked me not to hurry home so I can return the compliment
and not be too eager to rush back to the City and overdo things.[156]

About myself, there is nothing to report, you need not worry
about my condition, the grub is not all that it might be, nor
the time for going out sufficient and I shall not quite pick up
till I get back.

My cold is ever so much better and is probably due to the
change of climates, and being in a house once more after living
in the open air.

Ever your affectionate son

Frank

---

156 George Talley had been ill, and this was a cause of concern for his son.

20 October 1915

Mill Rd Hospital
Ward 3C
Liverpool

My dear Father

Your turn for a line this time, I had a note from May today
in which she says you have heard from Percy, I am sorry to hear
he is not A.1., but it is nice to know he is not in the fighting
line just now.

I have had very little particulars of him or the date of his
letter but reckon by this time a comfortable bed and good food
will have made a deal of difference to him.

The Doctor came round the ward this morning and gave me my
marching orders, I am not really sorry as it was getting dread-
fully monotonous up here and yet I did not want to do anything
to get sent away, fortunately things have taken their own course.

There is no news to give you, so will save up all details
until I see you on Saturday.

Ever your affectionate son

Frank

5 November 1915

My dearest Mother

Only a line to say that I am fixed here. There seems to be no chance of seeing a Dr, they simply make you fit and send you out with the first draft that goes; here we are only considered a nuisance. I have got a new rig out in everything from tunic and riding breeches down to a housewife.[157]

I shall wait for a day or two and see how things go & then consider what to do about the Commission business.[158] Taking things all round they are rotten and I feel a bit humpy, partly due I suppose from being away from you all my address is:

Tpr F.L. Talley 2365
C of L Yeomanry
Trefusis
West Hill
Putney

Please excuse more now as I still have a lot of odds and ends to do.

Yours

Frank

---

157 A 'housewife' or 'hussif' was a sewing kit, issued as part of the 'soldier's necessaries' to enable him to carry out repairs on his uniform where necessary.

158 Frank Talley was considering applying for a commission as a junior officer. His previous military experience, his education and the fact that he had survived the Dardanelles would all stand him in good stead. Losses amongst junior officers were high, and replacing them with suitable candidates was a struggle.

9 November 1915

'Trefusis'
West Hill
Putney

My dear Father

Only a line to let you know I am still O.K. and fairly comfortable; four 1st regiment men in our room are endeavouring
to get a smaller one to ourselves, but don't know whether we
shall succeed, but it will be very much nicer if we do.

I expect you have heard from Mabel of Mr Hain's suggestion
that I take a Commission in the Royal Engineers Signal Service.
I had not thought of this branch and shall decide later on when
I get the application form, this form will do for any branch of
the Service.

We have had a lovely day of rain, and an ideal one for the
show some of our fellows went from here to take part and
I believe some came down from Norfolk.

I wrote a good long letter to Percy yesterday, from what
I hear up here the division is likely to be sent, either
back to Egypt or to Servia,[159] in either case they will have
their horses.

Your affectionate son

Frank

---

159 Frank is referring to the situation in Salonika, facing the Bulgarians. The 10th Division
   left the peninsula in late September to move to the Greek city to take its place in the
   multinational force facing the new enemy.

23 November 1915

Trefusis
West Hill
Putney

My dearest Mother

Only a line to say I heard from Mr Hain this morning but
quite unsatisfactory. He sent me his letter to the Colonel and
the latter's reply, which was to the effect that I had to get
my C.O. to sign my application form, information which I could
have given him, so as far as I can see little help is likely
from this quarter. Another fellow and I went down to Woolwich
this morning to see if we could find out anything there but
only drew another blank.

We then introduced ourselves to the Father of one his friends,
who received us very well and is taking us down to Wood Green
tomorrow and introducing us to a friend of his a Major. I am
not expecting any results from the visit, but the unexpected
often happens and we will give it the chance, the appointment
is not until tomorrow night at 8 o'clock so will not be able to
let you know the result until Thursday.

I shall phone Tom in the morning as he said he knew a Colonel
who might do something for him, in the meantime I shall alter
my form to the R.F.A. as my previous four years may help me,
and I am losing time.

Love to all, yours

Frank

Frank Talley was indeed commissioned on 5 December 1915; he returned once
again to the 3rd London Brigade, Royal Field Artillery – the very unit he had
served with as a pre-war territorial. There is one surviving letter from his time
as a junior officer in Flanders. He served the rest of the war in the RFA, before
resigning his commission in 1919. One letter from this time survives:

9 November 1917

B.E.F

My dearest Wife

Your parcel arrived on Wednesday just as I was leaving for the gun line, so did not have time to open it until I got there, many thanks for the photograph case and the shaving mirror I did not laugh as you thought I might.

You will have read of our latest push and on account of it I had one of the liveliest days I have yet had. That is why I had to go up to the gun line, as I had to go over just after the infantry to try and keep up telephone communications. Needless to say it is about the most difficult job going as the wires were always cut by the shellfire, and then out we have to go and repair them. For 40 hours I existed on 1½ biscuits and my bottle of water, but I am glad to say I am back quite safely and down at the wagon line for a rest. I am hurrying this letter and shall try and get it stamped, and ride into the nearest mail office and get it away; as not having written for three days you may be getting anxious.

All love to you

Yours as ever

Frank

Frank and Percy Talley survived their time as Rough Riders. They served for just over a year. A year's service that was to take them from the windswept cliff tops of Norfolk, to the parched desert soils of Egypt, and the unrelenting battleground of Gallipoli.

In 1915, thirty-eight Rough Riders lost their lives in the service of their country, just over 10 per cent of the regiment. Many more were wounded, or became sick in the unhealthy conditions of the Gallipoli Peninsula. Of these thirty-eight, seventeen have their last resting places at Green Hill, facing their first and last objective; eight have no known grave on the peninsula. Others lie at Mudros, on the island of Lemnos, or at Suez, Malta or Gibraltar. Those who made it home, wounded, only to die there, lie in the quiet graveyard of an English church.

The Rough Riders went on to greater things. Returned to Egypt, they regained their beloved horses and were once again a mounted force operating in the Holy Land to great effect. And in the last stages of the war they would return with the Mounted Division to Europe, where they were committed to France in 1918. But the yeomanry would never forget that they took part in the last stand at Gallipoli, and the two brothers from Muswell Hill who joined their country's army.

John Hargrave of the RAMC, writing in 1916, expressed what must have been in the thoughts of all who left those fateful shores in autumn 1915:

Most of the accounts of marvellous escapes and acute encounters, secret scoutings and extraordinary expeditions will lie now for ever with the silent dead and the thousands of rounds of ammunition in the silver sand of Suvla Bay. The stars still burn above the Salt Lake bed, the breakers roll each morning along the blue sea-shore, sometimes washing up the bodies of the slain – just as they did when we camped near Lala Baba. But the guns are gone and there, the heavy silence of the waste places reigns supreme.[xiii]

Notes

i.   Ellis Ashmead-Bartlett, *The Times*, Saturday, 4 September 1915, p.7.
ii.   Liman von Sanders, *Five Years in Turkey*, 1928, p.89.
iii.   C.E. Callwell, *The Dardanelles*, 1924, p.254.
iv.   C.E. Callwell, *The Dardanelles*, 1924, p.255.
v.   Sir Charles Monro, quoted in C.F. Aspinall-Oglander, *Military Operations: Gallipoli, Vol. II*, p.403.
vi.   General Peyton, quoted in A.S. Hamilton, *The City of London Yeomanry (Rough Riders)*, 1936, p.61.
vii.   *Finchley Press*, Friday, 10 September 1915, p.6.
viii.   Ellis Ashmead-Bartlett, *The Times*, Saturday, 4 September 1915, p.7.
ix.   *Yorkshire Evening Telegraph & Star*, Tuesday, 14 December 1915, p.6, British Newspaper Archive.
x.   *Medical Report on an Invalid*, from Talley, P.L., Soldiers Service Records, The National Archives, Kew.
xi.   *Medical Report on an Invalid*, from Talley, P.L., Soldiers Service Records, The National Archives, Kew.
xii.   *Opinion of the Medical Board*, from Talley, P.L., Soldiers Service Records, The National Archives, Kew.
xiii.   John Hargrave, *At Suvla Bay*, 1916, pp.181–2.

Bibliography

The National Archives, Kew

Maps and plans, Suvla Bay area.
Soldiers' records, Percy L. Talley.
Soldiers' records, Frank L. Talley.
War Diary of the 2nd Mounted Division.

Newspapers

The Times.
Finchley Press.
Illustrated War News.

Published Works

Ashmead-Bartlett, E., *Despatches from the Dardanelles* (George Newnes, 1915).
Ashmead-Bartlett, E., *The Uncensored Dardanelles* (Hutchinson, 1928).
Ashurst, G., *My Bit. A Lancashire Fusilier at War, 1914–1918* (Crowood, 1987).
Aspinall-Oglander, C.F., *Military Operations: Gallipoli* (Heinemann, two volumes, 1929, 1932).
Bean, C.E.W., *Official History of Australia in the War of 1914–1918: The Story of Anzac* (Angus & Robertson, 2 volumes, 1938–42).
Behrend, A., *Make Me a Soldier: A Platoon Commander in Gallipoli* (Eyre & Spottiswoode, 1961).
Birdwood, Field Marshal Lord, *Khaki and Gown. An Autobiography* (Ward Lock & Co., 1941).
Callwell, C.E., *The Dardanelles* (Constable, 1924).
Carlyon, L., *Gallipoli* (Pan Macmillan, 2001).
Chasseaud, P. & Doyle, P., *Grasping Gallipoli. Terrain, Maps and Failure at the Dardanelles* (Spellmount, 2006).
Churchill, W.S., *The World Crisis 1911–1916* (Thornton Butterworth, 1931).
Cooper, B., *The Tenth (Irish) Division in Gallipoli* (Herbert Jenkins, 1918).
Crawley, R., *Climax at Gallipoli: The Failure of the August Offensive* (University of Oklahoma Press, 2014).

Creighton, O., *With the Twenty-Ninth Division in Gallipoli* (Longmans, Green & Co., 1916).

Dane, E., *British Campaigns in the Near East* (Hodder & Stoughton, 1918).

Doyle, P., *Gallipoli 1915* (Spellmount, 2011).

Gallishaw, J., *Trenching at Gallipoli* (A.L. Burt, 1916).

Hamilton, A.A., *The City of London Yeomanry (Rough Riders)* (Hamilton Press, 1936).

Hamilton, Sir I., *Ian Hamilton's Despatches from the Dardanelles* (George Newnes, 1917).

Hamilton, Sir I., *Gallipoli Diary* (Arnold, two volumes, 1920).

Hanna, H., *The Pals at Suvla Bay* (Ponsonby, 1917).

Hargrave, J., *At Suvla Bay* (Constable, 1916).

Hargrave, J., *The Suvla Bay Landing* (Macdonald, 1964).

Hart, P., *Gallipoli* (Profile, 2011).

Haythornthwaite, P.J., *Gallipoli 1915. Frontal Assault on Turkey* (Osprey, 1991).

Herbert, A., *Mons, Anzac and Kut* (Hutchinson, 1919).

Hickey, M., *Gallipoli* (John Murray, 1995).

James, R. Rhodes, *Gallipoli* (Batsford, 1965).

Lee, J., *A Soldier's Life: General Sir Ian Hamilton 1853–1947* (Macmillan, 2000).

Le Queux, W., *The Invasion of 1910* (George Newnes, 1906).

Liddle, P., *Men of Gallipoli* (Allen Lane, 1976).

McCombie, F., *Gallipoli: The Final Chance – General Kenna and the Yeomen at Suvla Bay* (University of Newcastle Upon Tyne, 1990).

Macleod, J., *Reconsidering Gallipoli* (Manchester University Press, 2004).

MacMunn, G., & C. Falls, *Military Operations, Egypt & Palestine* (HMSO, 1928).

Masefield, J., *Gallipoli* (Heinemann, 1916).

Mileham, P., *The Yeomanry Regiments* (Canongate Academic, 1985).

Moorhead, A., *Gallipoli* (Hamish Hamilton, 1956).

Moseley, S.A., *The Truth about the Dardanelles* (Cassell, 1916).

Murray, J., *Gallipoli as I Saw It* (William Kimber, 1965).

Nevinson, H.W., *The Dardanelles Campaign* (Nisbet & Co., 1918).

North, J., *Gallipoli, the Fading Vision* (Faber, 1936).

Ostler, W., *The Principles and Practice of Medicine* (Butterworth, 1916).

Prior, R., *Gallipoli: The End of the Myth* (Yale University Press, 2009).

Pugsley, C., *Gallipoli: The New Zealand Story* (Hodder & Stoughton, 1984).

Rogers, H.C.B., *The Mounted Troops of the British Army, 1066–1945* (Seeley Service, 1959).

Sanders, Liman von, *Five Years in Turkey* (Williams & Wilkins Co., 1928).

Snelling, S., *VCs of the Great War. Gallipoli* (Sutton, 1995).

Steel, N., & P. Hart, *Defeat at Gallipoli* (Macmillan, 1985).

Teichman, O., *The Diary of a Yeomanry M.O.* (Fisher Unwin, 1921).

Travers, T., *Gallipoli 1915* (Tempus, 2001).

Tyquin, M., *Gallipoli: The Medical War* (New South Wales University Press, 1993).

Waite, F., *The New Zealanders at Gallipoli* (Whitcombe & Tombs, 1921).

War Office, *The King's Regulations and Orders for the Army 1912* (HMSO, 1914).

War Office, *Manual of Military Law* (HMSO, 1914).

Wedgwood Benn, W., *In the Side Shows* (Hodder & Stoughton, 1919).

Westlake, R., *British Regiments at Gallipoli* (Leo Cooper, 1996).

Whitehead, J., *The Growth of Muswell Hill* (Jack Whitehead, 1985).

Wilkinson, N., *The Dardanelles* (Longmans, Green & Co., 1916).

Index